ESSENTIAL QUESTIONS
TO GROW
YOUR TEAM

By Kathryn Jackson of
www.careerbalance.co.nz

Essential Questions to GROW Your Team

Published by: Careerbalance Ltd

ISBN: 978-0-473-40495-6

BEFORE YOU GO ANY FURTHER...
WHY SHOULD YOU READ THIS BOOK?

There's no escaping the growth of interest in the power of coaching conversations at work.

No longer just the stuff of track and field, coaching questions are now proving to produce quicker results, increased accountability and (on many occasions) instantaneous personal development for the person being coached.

"Professional accountability, improved work performance, better time management, increased team effectiveness, enriched relationships, greater self-confidence, enhanced communication skills…and even a positive impact on business management."

These are all real benefits, quoted in an ICF study in collaboration with PriceWaterhouse Coopers 2013.

By using the coaching questions in this Book as a foundation for your conversations you will be able to:

- Develop a more self sufficient, solutions focussed and accountable team at work
- Have some of the difficult conversations at work with more confidence
- Help your team to get excited, motivated and more engaged at work
- Create bigger picture thinking or freshen up ideas in the people you work with

The book you are about to read has been designed to give you the tools to use coaching questions with everybody in your team, where you have decided that coaching is appropriate.

You can use the Conversation Guides as a framework to design your own questions, you can use them as a training tool or you can use them for your own self-coaching (like a reflective thinking framework).

Many of the conversations can take place in 10 minutes or less.

Global Reviews;

> "A vital guide to coaching conversations at work to deliver great business results"

Graham Alexander, founder of the Alexander Corporation, originator of the GROW model and author of SuperCoaching and Tales from the Top"

> "A brisk, no nonsense style book which will be truly helpful to people who want to coach their team"

Alison Hardingham – International Best-Selling author of eight books, and Director of Business Psychology at Yellow Dog Consulting UK**

> *** Alison has recommended Essential Questions for the Coach Training Programme that she delivers at Henley Business School, UK*

'Easily the best collection of coaching questions I've ever come across. As a professional coach whose clientele consists primarily of managers and executives, I know that I will be using many of the pages of this wonderful little book many, many times.' **Pierre Gauthier Certified Integral Coach (TM), Canada**

"This book has been an EXCEPTIONAL resource for the managers in my organisation and has totally changed the way that managers coach their people", **Alyson Howell, L&D Manager, New Zealand.**

'I currently use Essential Questions as a practical reference for my planning, preparation and running of both individual and team coaching sessions. It provides a brilliant "starter" template to build on – you can pick out the most relevant questions and then build your own. I can highly recommend Kathryn's work to anybody wishing to coach their team to higher performance'. **Stephanie Mohan, Team Coach, Singapore**

'As a mentor and coach to senior executives I can say that coaching is now an essential skill for them. Kathryn's book may be the start of or the inspiration to continue on this coaching journey, giving you practical tips to excel'. **Simon O'Shaughnessy, Executive and CEO Coach, Carista Ltd. New Zealand**

PART ONE

This part of the book contains a short introduction to help you decide who to coach (and who not to coach).

It then presents a series of some of the most common discussions at work, using the internationally acclaimed GROW model as a framework. These are called **Conversation Guides**.

Each Conversation Guide has been designed with questions using a coaching framework: Goal, Reality, Options and Will. It is recommended that to keep the conversation balanced, you select an equal number of questions from each section (for example, choose 3 questions from G, R, O, W. Do not choose one question from G, five from R, two from O and one from W).

The Conversation Guides have been designed as a quick example to review before you have a coaching discussion with a member of your team; they are intended for you to reshape and rewrite using your own words should you wish to do so.

Simply check that a coaching conversation is likely to be effective using the framework, select the most appropriate Conversation Guide, choose your questions and get started.

Alternatively, you can share the Conversation Guide with the person you want to coach, and ask them to select the questions they would like to discuss with you.

This is the main part of the book.

The Conversation Guides will be especially useful for:

- **Leaders and Managers who are new to coaching and want to practice before they have real discussions.**

- **All employees who like to think through what they want to say before a coaching conversation takes place.**

- **Trainers who are looking for materials to support their workshops.**

PART TWO

The second part of this book provides more detail on the origins and use of the GROW coaching model including a short overview of the following:

- The impact of learning preferences
- the core skills for coaching at work
- Some of the main barriers to coaching in the workplace

The book also includes a detailed reference section for further reading, including an overview of the main governing bodies for coaching around the world.

MEET THE AUTHOR

No doubt if you've found these books then you're eager to be the leader of a team that really knows how to self-perform, and you're interested in how coaching questions might play a key role in making that happen.

The idea for this work developed during the 11+ years I have been working as a full time Executive Coach and Leadership facilitator, based in Christchurch New Zealand.

Although there are plenty of exceptional resources to explain what coaching is, how to do it and list upon list of great coaching questions…I have found limited tools and resources to demonstrate how coaching questions might look in REAL conversations at work.

Leaders shared with me that they TOTALLY understood the concept of coaching, and the power that it brings with creating responsibility and accountability in their team – but they also wanted me to help them prepare for specific conversations at work, asking me what sort of questions might be helpful to ask and when.

I checked my experiences with other coaches around the world and they had a similar story…

…there was an opportunity for a simple, practical resource to highlight how GROW might sound in conversations at work.

As a result, the idea for these books was sown.

This book was first launched in 2010 as a PDF to support the Manager as Coach training workshops that I run. The feedback that I received was incredibly positive, and libraries and workplaces started asking me how they could purchase copies. The book you are currently reading is the result of that request.

Please feel free to adapt or change any questions you use from these books to make them sound more like something you would say. The Conversation Guides have been designed for you to read before having a coaching discussion, and then to use or adapt any of the questions that meet your needs. You might also choose to copy the conversation you plan to have, and encourage your team member to select their own questions, or at least do some preparation first.

The only thing I would ask is that you contact me if you'd like to publish or adapt any of the models that I've used because I've obtained special permissions to include them in my books, and would like to honour those permissions.

Thank you so much for investing your money in these books, I hope that you love them and find the information invaluable to your conversations in the workplace.

PS I'm absolutely delighted that you've chosen my book to help you out with your coaching conversations at work. While you're reading it, if you have any questions, or would like me to help you to design a coaching conversation that hasn't been included please don't hesitate to get in touch with me. I love growing this resource.

TABLE OF CONTENTS

PART ONE ESSENTIAL QUESTIONS

ON COACHING

Research by the Chartered Institute of Personnel & Development (CIPD Resourcing & Talent Planning Survey; UK, 2010) has highlighted that in-house development through coaching was the preferred way to grow skills, confidence and capability – used in 54% of the 500 organisations surveyed and compared with 36% in 2009.

The impact of and value in coaching at work is ever increasing.

There is widespread recognition that one management style does not suit all members of a team at all times, and while it is not appropriate to coach all of the time (just like it is not appropriate to "command and control" all of the time), there is an advantage to have coaching capability in all your managers' toolboxes so it can be used where necessary.

My purpose is not to create a book about "How to Coach" - there are already many great resources to achieve this, some of which are listed in the **Great Resources** section of the second chapter, GROW your team.

Before presenting the **Essential Questions** however, it is critical that we pause to explore some boundaries for when it is, and is not likely to be helpful to use coaching as a conversation style.

CAUTIOUS ENTHUSIASM

As a manager who had just been taught about the power of coaching conversations on a course, I returned to my team full of great ideas about questions and exciting notions of creating accountability and responsibility. I spent the next few weeks coaching my socks off; asking powerful coaching questions of everybody I met (including my poor, long suffering husband!).

I soon realised that this approach was not working, and when I looked at my 360-feedback report to check the impact of my coaching I started to see why;

> *"I sometimes wish Kathryn would not ask us a question every time - every now and then we just want advice!"*

> *"When Kathryn asks me a question that I don't know the answer to, it sometimes makes me feel stupid"*

> *"Kathryn used to be so helpful by providing solutions, now all she does is ask questions"*

I adapted my approach rapidly after reading this! I started asking questions like "would you like some coaching on this or are you looking for an immediate answer?". I also paid much closer attention to the non-verbal behaviours I saw to give me a clue about whether coaching might be the best solution.

Of course, sometimes I coached a little bit anyway, when I worked out that 'stealth coaching' can be a good tool for team members who like to take the easy way out by always asking for advice, when actually they could come up with some ideas of their own if they tried hard enough or were given some time to think.

DECIDING WHO TO COACH

A simple way to decide whether it would be appropriate to ask a coaching question is to ask yourself how much knowledge the person is 'likely' to have about the subject.

I have deliberately written 'likely' because you're never going to be 100% sure unless you ask the other person.

For example, let's say you are talking with a new manager who's just moved into a role where you know they are managing a team for the first time and you ask them for their ideas on **Options** for approaching a conversation with somebody who's underperforming.

It's unlikely that the new manager will be able to do more than guess a response…and that might seem a bit uncomfortable or risky for them especially as they probably want to make a good impression on you and seem knowledgeable in their role!

However, you could ask the same manager whether they have ever handled a performance management conversation before, or heard a performance management conversation handled well by another person.

Using their response, you can decide whether to **Tell More or Ask More**.

- **Tell More** - If the response is that they <u>have not</u> handled or experienced this before, you could adopt a more **Instructive** style; pointing out some of the risks, encouraging them to speak to Human Resources, showing them where the resources are to help them and checking the support they need from you. You've chosen this style because their knowledge, skills and experience in handling discussions about performance is LOW. You might still ask some coaching style questions, but most of your conversation will be sharing information that you know.

- **Ask More** - If the response is that they <u>have</u> handled or experienced an underperformer before, you could adopt a more **Encouraging** or **Coaching** style; encouraging them to remember the main content of the discussion, outcomes they achieved, challenges they overcame and subsequently plan how they will approach this conversation. You've chosen this style because their knowledge, skills and experience in handling discussions about performance is HIGH.

COACHING CONTINUUM

The **Coaching Continuum Model** is a framework to help you decide whether coaching is likely to be helpful by highlighting that the level of knowledge, skills or experience of your team member should dictate whether it would be appropriate to be more instructive in your approach, or whether a more enabling coaching style would be preferable.

Coaching Continuum		
Low	**Team Member Capability** (knowledge, skills, experience)	High
Instruct Inform Advise	Challenge	Expand Encourage
Tell More (be directive)		**Ask More** (be enabling)

(**If you'd like me to acknowledge this as your Coaching Continuum please contact me as I cannot find a source for this model. I believe it draws from Situational Leadership, Blanchard et al 1985)

TRAFFIC LIGHTS

An alternative framework for you to use when deciding to coach would be the **Traffic Light Model** – which I designed in collaboration with one of my New Zealand clients.

We were exploring the impact of **Motivation** and **Skill** on whether a team member would be appropriate to coach, and the **Traffic Light Model** represents the conclusions that we drew for my client.

Please feel free to adapt this model for your own workplace.

Skill Low **Motivation High** (coach with caution) AMBER	**Skill High** **Motivation High** (coach with caution) AMBER
Skill Low **Motivation Low** (Avoid coaching) RED	**Skill High** **Motivation Low** (Best for coaching) GREEN

RED

Our conclusions were that coaching somebody who has low skill AND low motivation might not get you very far. These were defined as the team members that perhaps don't have the ability to perform well in their role, <u>and</u> they also don't show any sort of motivation about their work.

We concluded that they may even be in the wrong job and that encouraging them to move into new areas of responsibility might improve their motivation or lead them to use skills that they are more confident in using – but until that time our conclusion was that it might be unkind to coach them at all.

We discussed whether it would be more appropriate for an external (and therefore independent) coach to work with this team member to encourage them to regain their enthusiasm for work, and concluded that the most important outcome for this group was a clear understanding of what was expected of them at work – perhaps using more of a formal performance feedback and guidance based approach.

AMBER

Where team members have high motivation (regardless of whether they are highly skilled or not), we concluded that it would be appropriate to coach them – but with caution.

 For real 'high flyers' in the team (those with high skill, high motivation) we concluded that coaching can sometimes be incredibly beneficial to encourage them towards the next level of their capabilities…but that used inappropriately, or by a well-meaning but inexperienced leader, coaching might result in them believing that their capability was being called into question, or that deficiencies were being identified.

We believed one of the most important factors in coaching this group would be to clearly explain why coaching was being used as a development tool – perhaps exploring how it will support their career to an even higher level. It is also imperative that they choose to be coached, possibly even selecting an external coach to help challenge and develop their capabilities.

For the 'enthusiastic' members of your team that don't quite have the skills but are loving their job (the low skill, high motivation group), we wondered whether coaching might accidentally curb that enthusiasm, so concluded that a more directive approach might be more appropriate, unless the manager or leader was a very careful coach.

Within my client's workplace, this enthusiastic style was typical for new members of the team who were looking for clarity on what was expected of them and ideas for how to work effectively in their new workplace and coaching questions might just highlight what they don't know. We did however conclude that questions might encourage them to look for answers if used sensitively.

GREEN

The conclusion we reached for my client was that the best team members for using the GROW coaching model with would be those who are highly skilled and capable but have perhaps lost their motivation, or their confidence at work or who maybe are not making decisions for themselves.

We decided that coaching might help this group to regain their self-confidence and challenge their own self-limiting beliefs, thereby encouraging them to take new actions and start to believe that they can achieve even more through their work and their career.

Some ideas we had for how these people might look included; capable team members who often stayed late or missed deadlines, people approaching retirement, employees without a clear career plan – and who have been in a similar role for a while, team members who don't speak up in meetings and those who were reluctant to make decisions.

We also concluded that sometimes these Green team members can be labelled the 'trouble makers' in that by being highly skilled but without the motivation they may use those skills in all the wrong directions.

THE HAWTHORNE EFFECT

From 1924-1932 a study was conducted at the Hawthorne Works (a Western Electric manufacturing facility outside Chicago). The study was to see if its workers would become more productive in higher or lower levels of light.

Quite simply, the conclusions of the study were that regardless of higher or lower levels of light, the workforce productivity improved when changes were made...and then slumped when the study was concluded.

The very fact that there was interest and focus in their productivity levels became an incentive to achieve more.

This study became one of the earliest Workplace Motivation studies and is also sometimes known as the 'Someone Upstairs Cares' effect.

It's worth reflecting on what this means for taking the time to focus on your team by using Essential Questions to explore their experience at work.

By talking to them about "them", not about business deadlines, job updates and deadlines you will demonstrate that you care about them. You will show that you want to support them in their work, and therefore you are likely to see more engagement and commitment to your outcomes as a result.

Use the following model to think through your own team members using the Red, Amber and Green Categories to help you identify whether a coaching conversation might be appropriate. Be very careful if you write anything down – without context it could be seriously misinterpreted if discovered on the printer ☺

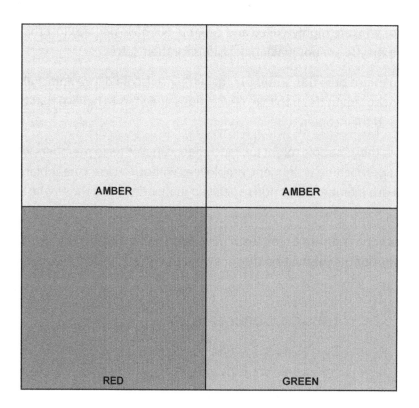

For the team members you will not be coaching, how will you work with them instead to ensure that organisational goals are still achieved?

Who will support you in having discussions or taking action?

What will you do to help them get back on track –with increased skills and capability or a more motivated approach at work?

THE ESSENTIAL QUESTIONS

The next part of this book is dedicated to **Essential Questions** and includes a summary of some of the main conversations that can take place in the workplace, with questions mapped back to the GROW model.

On each page, there is a series of GROW questions for you to work with and develop into your own, and you'll also see a reminder of the GROW model that we are using, so that you can easily check that your coaching discussion is covering the whole framework – remembering to keep checking in with the **Goal** along the way!

In addition, there's a space for you at the end of this chapter to add your own **Great Coaching Questions** – perhaps you've heard somebody use it and kept it tucked away for your own personal use. I've included some favourites to get you started.

Use the GROW framework to check that your own questions are covering the **Goal**, **Reality**, **Options** and **Will**… and not just all focussed in one area.

How to use the Conversation Guides:

1. Reflect on a conversation you need to have at work. Find the Conversation Guide that matches it.

2. Check that coaching will likely be appropriate (use the Coaching Continuum or Traffic Light model)

3. Read through the questions for each section G.R.O.W

4. Choose two or three questions from each section G.R.O.W (or adapt to include the words you would prefer to use) *Try to keep the conversations "balanced" – don't pick one G question, two R questions, five O questions and one W question!

5. Consider sharing the questions in advance of your meeting; feedback from readers of this book has suggested they can give precious time to team members who like to think about what they want to say.

6. Have the conversation.

7. Reflect on the conversation; review what went well, where you weren't so comfortable, how the person you were coaching responded to your questions and what you'd like to do different next time.

Remember that to find out more about the GROW Model – how it was developed, how to use it, what it means etc. you should read the second chapter in this book…GROW Your Team.

CREATING PERFORMANCE OBJECTIVES

It's typical to take some time each year to create personal objectives for your team which are aligned with the overall business objectives of the organisation. Often the two are considered very separately with the result that individuals don't clearly see how their own actions impact business success. Even more common is that performance objectives for individuals are 'set' by the leader, with very little consideration to what employees really want to achieve at work.

Coaching questions can help your team to consider how their own skills, knowledge and experience can contribute to achieving the organisation goals, and identify possible performance goals that are aligned.

It can be helpful to understand the personal values and motivators in your team for this discussion to support a more meaningful discussion about how they 'fit' into the organisation. It is essential that you are familiar with the latest business objectives, and that you have shared them with your team before this discussion.

G GOAL	• What does your overall focus at work need to be for you to meet the needs of the business, but also to really enjoy your job? • Which specific business targets interest you the <u>most</u>? Explore • Which specific business targets interest you the least? Explore • What will the achievement of this business objective mean to you personally? • How could achieving that business objective result in you having more XYZ at work (insert values, skills or motivators)? • Where do we as a team need to prioritise to ensure business success? • What are the top five priorities to you currently in your work?
R REALITY	• How does your current role or responsibilities directly contribute to the overall goals of the organisation? • What would need to change in your current role or responsibilities to enable you to contribute more directly to the achievement of this business goal? • To what extent does your role currently allow you to have XYZ (insert values, skills or motivators) • For the business targets that interest you the most, how does your current role enable you to contribute to them? • What stops you from contributing to the business targets that interest you the most? • Which of your top five priorities could have the biggest impact on our organisation?
O OPTIONS	• What ideas do you have about knowledge, skills or abilities that you'd like to develop over the next 12 months to support the achievement of our business goals? • How could we formally record your personal performance objectives so that they are aligned to the formal business objectives of the business? • What different options would you have within the organisation to develop your knowledge, skills and abilities to contribute even further to the business goals? • Who has already contributed widely to this business goal or has the skills to provide you with some mentoring along the way?
W WILL	• How will you chart your progress against achieving the performance goals that we have agreed today? • How will we measure your success against achieving those objectives? • What action do you need to take on a daily/weekly/monthly basis to achieve your goals? • What support do you need from me to achieve these goals?

COACHING UNDER PERFORMANCE

During your career as a leader you may occasionally be required to discuss under-performance with members of your team. Taking into consideration the capability and wider performance of the employee involved will be crucial to help you to decide if a coaching conversation is appropriate – please refer to the **Coaching Continuum Model** and the **Traffic Light Model** to do this.

For example, if your employee does not have the knowledge or capability to deliver the work that was required of them, then coaching might not be appropriate. Similarly, if the poor performance is part of a wider pattern of under delivery then it may be more appropriate to initiate formal performance management processes with the support of your Human Resources team.

You may also wish to explore some models for **Giving Feedback** to support your discussion about under performance at work –searching the internet will identify models like the EEC model (Example, Effect, Change/Consequence), the TELL Model (Tell, Explain, Listen, Let Know) and the old faithful (and often maligned) Sandwich Model.

Once you have identified that a coaching conversation could be helpful, here are some questions you might use;

G **GOAL**	• Let's talk about that project you delivered last week – what were some of the key things you were hoping to achieve? • When you consider how you're delivering against your performance objectives, how do you think you're doing? • What sort of feedback have you had from your leaders about the work you've delivered this year? • We need to talk about what happened in that client meeting this morning – what was your thinking behind the comments that you shared?
R **REALITY**	• If they were the key things that you wanted to achieve, to what extent do you think you achieved them? • The feedback that I've been hearing from people working with you has been that you are not achieving your goals in the following areas; XYZ (be specific) • It sounds as though while there are one or two areas that are going well, there are some specific areas you think you are struggling with? Explore. • It seems that the thinking behind sharing those comments in the client meeting was to share XYZ information – how well do you think you did that? • What impact could that have on your results/the business/the team?
O **OPTIONS**	• What ideas do you have for addressing the specific areas that aren't working out for you? • I'd like to share some thoughts on actions you could take to get back on track – would that be helpful? • What might get in the way and prevent you from further achieving? How could you overcome them? • What's stopping you from achieving your objectives right now? • Who do you need to talk to and what are they key things you need to tell them or share?
W **WILL**	• What do you plan to do next to get back on track? What's the first step you need to take? • When would you like to achieve that by? • What support would you like from me? • When shall we get together to check in on how that's going? • I'd like to provide you with full support on that, let's meet at the end of the day/as appropriate to find out how things are going.

CREATING CAREER GOALS

Having a regular discussion with each team member about their career goals is vital in any organisation. This can help to create a mutual understanding of their career values, motivators and the skills that they would like to use or develop while working with your business.

There is enormous power in these discussions, because they can help team members understand that you have a personal interest in supporting their career development. However, this doesn't necessarily mean that they must constantly climb the career ladder – stretching more and more each year.

People will look for different things from their career throughout their lives; perhaps cutting back on stress and responsibilities at work for a while for one reason or another. Or they might not. It's a very personal thing. Managing expectations **realistically** is one of the most important roles you can play in this discussion – ensuring that they have a reasonable understanding of the opportunities that could be available to them in your organisation, and their current ability to achieve in future roles – while encouraging and supporting their plans to get there.

G GOAL	• What is your overall goal for your career? • When you think about what you'd like to be doing in 2/5/10yrs time, what does it look like? • How will you know when you've achieved your latest career goals? • What have been your proudest moments in your career so far? • What is the most important thing about work to you? • When you think back, how did you hope your career would work out for you? • What were some of the main reasons that you accepted this job?
R	• What do you really love about your job right now? • What would you like to change about your job right now? • How does your current job compare with your vision of what you'd like to be doing? • Are there any skills that you would like to use more often? Or less frequently? • Is there anything that you need to change to get where you'd like to go with your career? • What has been getting in the way of achieving your career goals so far?
O	• What ideas do you have for ways that you could change your job to make it more enjoyable? • What other roles or opportunities do you see in the organisation or industry that you would like to find out more about? • How could you develop your knowledge, skills and abilities to bring them more into line with the knowledge, skills and abilities that you will need in your future career? • Who do you know that's already doing that sort of job? What could you do to find out more about how they got there? What would you want to know from them? • What ideas do you have for how we could work together to ensure that you can use your XYZ skills more (or less)?
W WILL	• What would you like to achieve in the next 12 months to take you closer to this career goal? • Who could help you to achieve these things? • What might get in the way? How will you overcome it? • What are the consequences if you don't take steps towards achieving your career goals? • What support do you need, and from whom? • When would you like to have achieved your career goals? • What are you going to do first?

DEBRIEFING A PROJECT

When a significant piece of work has been delivered it can be useful to consider how things went. This can help to raise awareness around what went well and therefore could be continued, or taken into new projects. It can also help to identify what hasn't gone to plan, with a view to identifying lessons learned or exploring root causes that need addressing.

For projects that span a considerable length of time you could consider having this sort of conversation at regular intervals, rather than waiting until the end.

You should make an informed decision on whether you would like to hold this conversation with individuals or with the project team, depending on the circumstances.

G GOAL	• I'd like to review how the XYZ project went – what were our overall aims in delivering it? • In delivering phase two of this project, what were some of the main results we needed? • What were the key outcomes we were looking for? • What were the overall constraints that we wanted to overcome? • Who were the major competitors that we wanted to outperform? • Who were the main people we wanted to influence? • What outcomes had we committed to with our clients?
R REALITY	• On reflection, to what extent did we meet our aims? • I'd like to share my own thoughts on how well we achieved against our deliverables – SHARE EXAMPLES • How well do we believe those outcomes were achieved? • I'd like you to share your ideas on how well we achieved that. • On a scale of 1-10, how well did we influence those people? • Was there anything that didn't go to plan? • What were some of the key lessons that we learned? • Were there any deadlines or milestones that we missed? What ideas do you have about why we missed them?
O OPTIONS	• What ideas do you have for additional action we need to take to ensure that our overall aims are achieved or achieved next time? • How could we get things back on track? • If we were doing this project again, from the start – what would we do differently? • What do we need to change about this sort of project in the future? • What else could we include next time? • What action could we take in the future? • What are the really great things that we achieved that could be applied to other projects? • Are there any similar projects in the organisation that might benefit from our learning?
W WILL	• What are we specifically committing to do after this meeting? • Who is going to take ownership of XYZ actions? • When are we going to achieve this by? • What will we do to overcome obstacles? • Who else needs to be involved in our plans? • What support do you need from me as the overall leader of this project?

IDENTIFYING MOTIVATORS

As a manager, it can be very helpful to understand the different things that motivate your team, so that you can encourage them and support them in achieving their best. Whether you're operating in a strong economy or a recession, an understanding of WHY people have chosen to work with your business can help you to give them more responsibilities that play to those motivations.

A review of the research on motivation will show that money is very rarely a motivator at work; often the leaders in an organisation have very little say on how much money is allocated, and where - so it can be valuable to focus on other areas over which you have more control.

It's likely that your team will be motivated by one or more of the following; Expertise, Balance, Security, Contribution, Business Creation, Influence, Independence and Challenge.

I use an awesome Online Career Centre to help people more scientifically identify what motivates them at work and why. It's available globally, is used across a wide range of industries and can be tailored for your business. Connect with the team at www.Fuel50.com and tell them I sent you .

G GOAL	• What are the main things that you enjoy when you're doing your job here? • What do you love most about working here? • Have you ever had a job where you found that you were passionate about working there? What was it about that job that you loved? • Tell me about the last time you had an amazing day at work. • When do you feel at your most energised in work? • (If you know the Motivator) What does that (Motivator) mean to you? • Outside of work, what are you <u>really</u> passionate about? What drives that passion?
R REALITY	• To what extent does your current role allow you to do or experience that? • How does your amazing day at work differ to your normal days? • In your current role, how much of that (Motivator) are you getting? • What was different about the job that you passionately enjoyed? How was it different to your current role? • In a previous role, what has excited you or motivated you about work? • What would need to change in your job for it to be more enjoyable? • To what extent are you experiencing (Motivator) in your current role?
O OPTIONS	• What changes would we need to make to your current role to bring it closer to that description? • If you could make three changes to your work so it's more enjoyable for you what would they be? • What ideas do you have for making your job more enjoyable for you? • How could you make changes to your role or how you deliver your role to make it more motivational for you? • What jobs have you seen which you think you COULD be passionate about? • Who or what might be impacted by that, and how could we overcome it?
W WILL	• What do you want to change immediately? • What are you going to change in the next 12 months? • What action are you going to take? • Who else do you need to talk to or seek support from? • How could we work together to make that happen? • What support do you need from me? • When are we going to get back together to check our progress?

DISCUSSING VALUES AT <INSERT EMPLOYER>

Igniting a passion for work doesn't come from setting objectives or dishing out tasks, it comes from learning what your team values about what they do and how they do it.

Organisation values can set an organisation apart from others as a place to work, but without depth and wider understanding they can become a meaningless statement of intent, or worse they can undermine business performance if non-adherence is tolerated.

Workplace values are often designed to drive the "how" of the way we deliver our promises to clients, to colleagues and to ourselves. By taking time to understand how your team interprets these values you are more likely to help them bring values to life at work, and make them meaningful.

G GOAL	<ul><li>The <insert employer> Values are: ABCDEF Which of these values appeals to you the most?</li><li>What's your favourite of the <insert employer> values? Explore</li><li>What's your least favourite of the <insert employer> values? Explore</li><li>Which value are you focussing most of your energy on?</li><li>What does <insert Value ABCDEF> mean to you personally?</li><li>What is it like when you are 100% <insert value: ABCDEF>?</li><li>What examples have you seen at <insert employer> of where we are being 100% true to our values?</li><li>What examples have you noticed where we are letting our values down?</li><li>Are there any values that you don't believe in, or don't subscribe to? Explore.</li><li>What do you think is the main reason that these are our values at <insert employer>? What are the driving forces behind making them a priority?</li><li>To what extent do our values demonstrate who we are right now, vs what we want to be in the future?</li><li>How do we know that our commitment to <insert value: ABCDEF> is better than any other company?</li><li>What questions do you have about our core values at <insert employer>?</li><li>If you had to focus on bringing to life just one value, what would you choose? Explore.</li><li>I'd like to share my thoughts on how our core values at <insert employer> influence the work we do, and am keen to explore how my views compare with yours.</li></ul>
R REALITY	<ul><li>How is your definition or interpretation of the value different from the definition used by <insert employer>?</li><li>How is your definition or interpretation of the value the same as the definition used by <insert employer>?</li><li>To what extent are you able to use these/this value at work right now?</li><li>How are you bringing this value to life at work in your job?</li><li>If you are not prioritising a value, what impact is this having on you?</li><li>What's the most <insert value: ABCDEF> thing you've ever done while working (at <insert employer> or at another company).</li><li>How are the values currently rewarded and encouraged at <insert employer> or in your job?</li><li>What examples are there where values are being undermined or diluted?</li><li>What am I currently doing to help you lean into the <insert employer> values at work?</li><li>How are values currently brought to life through our employment lifecycle at <insert employer>?</li><li>How do you use the <insert employer> values to support (or dispute) decision making in your role?</li><li>What is your favourite story of the impact a value has had on you, or on something that <insert employer> has achieved?</li><li>What is currently getting in the way of you leaning into these/this value at work right now?</li><li>What might be the dark side of our values? How will we recognise if our commitment to them is adversely affecting our business performance?</li><li>To what extent have you been able to prioritise these/this values so far?</li><li>How do my thoughts about <insert employer> values at work compare with your thoughts?</li></ul>

O **OPTIONS**	• What ideas do you have for leaning further into <insert value: ABCDEF> to bring it alive for you? • What opportunities are there for values to be more deeply embedded into <insert employer>? • What ideas do you have for <insert employer> to promote values even more within the organisation or externally to customers and suppliers? • What impact could it have on you or your work if you were to lean into/dial up % <insert value: ABCDEF> in your job? • What are the different ways that you could create the opportunity for these/this value in your work? • For those values which you don't subscribe to, how can we make sure this doesn't stop you from doing a really great job? • What ideas do you have for bringing these/this value to life within our team? What impact could this have? • When have you seen this value brought to life in other organisations? What could we learn from this? • How could we adapt or grow the values which are not supporting our business goals at <insert employer>? • What could you do to regain that sense of <insert Value ABCDEF>? • How could we remove the barriers which prevent <insert Value ABCDEF>?
W **WILL**	• What are you going to do because of this discussion? • What can I help you with? • Who else do we need to involve? • How can we get the support we need to achieve this or explore it further? • When could that realistically be achieved? • What could be the first step that you take towards making that happen? • What will have changed when you've achieved it? • What are you committed to do to make that happen? • What could go wrong along the way? How will we handle this? • What might get in the way? How will you overcome it? • To what extent will this address your overall goal? • What support would you like from me?

CREATING BETTER WORK-LIFE BALANCE

I don't like the term work-life balance for many reasons. Occasionally there may be times when you notice that a member of your team is working extra-long hours – perhaps they are always in the office when you arrive, or stay late after most people have left for the night. Sometimes it's because we're doing something we're passionate about…

If this is unusual behaviour, or seems to be causing distress then a quick discussion might help to resolve what's going on. If this is a pattern behaviour then a more detailed coaching discussion might get to the heart of what's going on or HR support may be required.

While poor work-life balance may be an indication of wider (and sometimes personal) issues, it is still a great opportunity to explore what's going on…and find out whether there are any changes that could be made to responsibilities; to managing workload; or to some other factor that is impacting their ability to leave the office or focus on their work.

G **GOAL**	• On a scale of 1-10 how happy are you with your work life balance right now? • I've noticed for the past few weeks/days that you've been working particularly long hours, could you tell me a little more about what's going on for you right now? • When we last met you mentioned that you were keen to make changes to your work-life balance, how's that going for you now? • If I could wave a magic wand and give you a perfect work-life balance, what would that look like? • What does having a great work-life balance mean to you?
R **REALITY**	• What is getting in the way of you having a perfect 10/10 work-life balance? • How do you like to spend your time when you're not in the office? • How would you prefer to be spending your time? • Is there a specific part of your work that's causing your work-life balance issues? Explore • How will you know when you're happy with your work-life balance? What will be different? • How does your definition of great work-life balance compare with what's really going on for you?
O **OPTIONS**	• Has there ever been a time when you had a great work-life balance? Explore • What ideas do you have about things that would need to change in order to improve your work-life balance? • What have you already tried to change? How did that go for you? • Who seems to have a similar workload or responsibilities but a great work-life balance? What do they do differently? • What different ways can you think of to address each of the challenges that you have with your work-life balance?
W **WILL**	• What is the first step that you need to take towards having a better work-life balance? • When do you want to achieve this by? • If you were to take just one step towards improving your work-life balance, what would that be? • What will you commit to doing differently over the next week/month to try to address some of the work-life balance issues you have identified? • Who could help you to achieve a better work-life balance? • What support do you need from me?

COACHING FOR OVER OR UNDER UTILISATION

One of the challenges with managing time and resource at your organisation may be to ensure that utilisation targets are as closely met as possible.

Both over and under allocation can result in significant issues, and often requires an honest discussion about what is going on for your team member.

Over allocation may be due to a variety of things including poor time management, lack of ability or clarity about required results and can result in poor standards of work, or stressed out team members. Under allocation may be because of mismatched skills or personality clashes and can result in team members being avoided for team selection or perceived as lacking in the skills required. The result of both is often severely demotivated people in your team and often adversely affected business results.

The same sort of questions can be applied for other business targets, like sales targets or call targets.

G GOAL	• Tell me what you understand about the organisations (and your) utilisation targets. • What is your target utilisation figure for the current year? • What would be the overall impact of achieving your utilisation targets on the business? On you personally? • Having reviewed your latest utilisation figures, it seems that you are over/under target – I'd like a discussion about how to help get you back on track • I've noticed that you are under/over utilised in your workload currently and want to explore why that might be the case, and help you to get back on track. Can you tell me more about it?
R REALITY	• Talk me through your current utilisation figures – tell me how things are going for you in your work overall. • How do your current utilisation figures compare with the plan for your utilisation? • Is there anybody in the organisation or your team, who has a utilisation target that you aspire to achieving? • What is getting in the way of you achieving your target utilisation? • Is there anybody in the organisation or your team who has similar responsibilities and is achieving their utilisation targets? What are they doing differently? Explore. • What is the current overall utilisation rate for the project or projects that you are working on? Explore. • Has there ever been a time when you achieved your utilisation target? Explore.
O OPTIONS	• What ideas do you have for ways that we can work together to increase/decrease your utilisation figures? • Who could you talk to for more information about increasing/decreasing your utilisation figures? • What other projects could be influenced by a change in your utilisation rate? • What do you believe are the main reasons that you are over/under utilised currently? • What options are there for us to explore your current responsibilities to get your utilisation target back on track?
W WILL	• What action can you take right now to get closer to your target utilisation figures? • Who do you need to talk to increase/decrease your utilisation • How can we ensure that you are back on track within one month/two months/six months? • What specific responsibilities need to change in the next week/month to get you back on track to achieve your utilisation target?

COACHING TO ENCOURAGE INVOLVEMENT

As a leader, there may be times when a member of your team doesn't want to contribute to the team (or feels they can't). This can be due to many reasons, which they may or may not choose to share.

If this is unusual behaviour, there may have been an event or action that has resulted in them withdrawing from the group and a coaching conversation could help to resolve this.

If they have never really been involved with the team, then this could be a good opportunity to find out more about the team dynamic, or the personal communication preferences of your team member – perhaps they would prefer to share ideas with you before the meeting, or may want time to reflect on decisions outside the meeting room.

G GOAL	<ul><li>In our team meetings, I've noticed that sometimes you seem very thoughtful, but often choose not to share your thoughts. Can you tell me a bit about what's going on for you right now?<ul><li>I've noticed that over the last (X) weeks/months/days you've been less involved in the team activities and I wanted to check that everything's OK?</li><li>When we have one-to-one meetings, I've noticed that you have some great ideas for our team, but at our team meeting you seem reluctant to share them. Could you tell me what causes you to be reluctant?</li><li>I've seen you have great conversations with your team mates about your ideas for our projects, but when it comes to sharing those ideas you prefer to back down – can you tell me what causes that to happen?</li><li>That sounds like a great idea and I'd love to share that with our team – how would you like us to do that?</li></ul></li></ul>
R REALITY	<ul><li>What happens when you find yourself wanting to share an idea or thought that you've had?</li><li>Has this ever happened before?</li><li>What would we need to change about our meetings so that you feel more comfortable with sharing your ideas and thoughts?</li><li>Has there ever been a time when you felt able to share your ideas and thoughts? Explore<ul><li>On a scale of 1-10, how comfortable do you feel about sharing your thoughts and ideas during our team meetings?</li></ul></li><li>What seems to stop you from sharing your thoughts and ideas with the team?</li><li>Can you think of a time when you've shared an idea or thought with the team? What happened?</li></ul>
O OPTIONS	<ul><li>What ideas do you have for how we could change our team meetings so that you feel more comfortable with sharing your ideas and thoughts?</li><li>What might be the different benefits or outcomes of sharing your ideas and thoughts in our team meetings?</li><li>What ideas do you have for different things you'd like to get involved with supporting?</li><li>If you were in charge of our team meetings, how would you like to change them?</li><li>How have you shared your ideas in other or previous jobs?</li><li>How might your current approach to our team meetings impact you in the future?</li></ul>
W WILL	<ul><li>What role would you like me to play in supporting you to achieve this?</li><li>What support would you like from me to make that happen?</li><li>Who do you need to talk to in order to make this happen?</li><li>What would be the first step that you'd like to take?</li><li>What are you going to do?</li><li>When would you like to do that by?</li></ul>

EXPLORING TALENTS

When you have any sort of development discussion with the members of your team, it's highly likely that you will want to help them to identify the knowledge, skills and experience that they bring to their role.

In doing so, your team may form ideas about knowledge, skills and experience they would like to develop, or those that they would like to avoid using – perhaps identifying others in your team who have an interest and inclination towards using those skills instead. This can often give you a great opportunity to ensure the growth and development of other team members, while re-igniting the drive of those who are changing their responsibilities.

A simple way to do this can be to ask them to consider skills they like/don't like and skills they are competent/not competent in within a 2x2 matrix. Consider using the Job Description as a starting point.

G GOAL	• What are the main skills/talents that you enjoy using in your job? • What do you believe are your strongest skills/talents? • When you're doing your job, which skills do you enjoy using the most? • Are there any skills/talents that you are not currently using in your job, but which you'd like to use? Explore. • What skills/talents have you used in previous roles that you'd like to use more of in your current job? • Are there any skills/talents that you are using which you do not enjoy? Explore • Are there any skills/talents which you enjoy using and you'd like to get better at?
R REALITY	• To what extent are you able to use those skills in your job right now? • Have you ever been in a role where you were able to use those skills/talents before? Explore. • How often do you use those skills/talents in your job now? • How good are you currently on a scale of 1-10 at using those skills/talents? • How good on a scale of 1-10 would you like to be? What would need to change to get you closer to 10/10?
O OPTIONS	• What ideas do you have for ways to increase your ability to use those skills in your job? • What ideas do you have for other ways that we can get the same result, but perhaps without using your skills/talents? • How have you used these skills/talents previously? Explore. • What could we do to change your role so that you can use those skills/talents more (or less)? • Who else do you think would be better placed to use those skills/talents? • What ideas do you have for developing those skills/talents? • Who do you know that's great at using that skill/talent and what could you learn from them? • What might be the impact of moving those skills/talents elsewhere?
W WILL	• What are you going to do to develop those skills/talents? • When would you like to do it by? • Who do we need to get buy in and support from to achieve that? • How are you/we going to measure your success? • What support do you need from me? • Who else could help you? • What action are you going to take? • What could you do right now? • What would you like to achieve in the next 12 months?

GETTING READY FOR RETIREMENT

A coaching conversation can help people approaching the end of their "traditional" working life to explore what retirement means to them, and how you can support them as they step out of their current working world, and an early planning discussion with you could help to ensure as smooth a transition as possible – for many their concept of "retirement" is totally different to our preconceived ideas.

Helping them in this way may prevent some of the fear that can sometimes accompany a transition from being a <insert job description> to being "just a retiree", or may prevent your team member from simply drifting towards their "golden years" without preparation. Look for ways of creating a positive and legacy leaving transition.

G GOAL	• What are you most looking forward to about retirement? Explore. • Is there anything that you're not looking forward to? Explore. • I want to check that you're aware of the company retirement policy which is XYZ. How can I best support you in preparing for your own retirement from this role? • What does being retired mean to you? • Tell me about your retirement plans. Explore • I've noticed that recently your approach at work has changed (outline the change – good or bad, be specific) – and I'd like to talk about the impact that it's having. • What are your plans over the next 2+yrs as you approach the point where we need to discuss your retirement plans? • What is the legacy that you'd like to leave with the organisation? How would you like your work to be remembered? • What is retirement going to free you up to do?
R REALITY	• How much of that (what you're most/least looking forward to) are you doing now? • How does your current experience at work match up to those plans? • What might get in the way of achieving your retirement plans? • How does your work currently compare with these plans for retirement? • How might that approach be impacting the team? Or affecting the business? • What are some of the biggest risks that our business faces when you retire? • Who are the retirement role models for you? • Where do your beliefs about retirement come from?
O OPTIONS	• What ideas do you have for ways to stay focussed and motivated as you approach your retirement date? • What ideas do you have about overcoming those things? • Do you know anybody who has achieved that? Explore. • What resources or people might be able to support you? • What other options might there be to you retiring? • How else might you be able to use the skills and experience that you've gained? • What ideas do you have to re-ignite or start the hobbies and interests that you'd like to do more of in retirement? • Who else on the team might be interested in taking on more responsibility in that area?
W WILL	• What do you need to do to ensure that you're able to do that by the time you retire? • When would you like that to happen? • What is the first step that you could take towards that? • How would you like me to help you to achieve that? • What are you going to do?

COACHING A WORKPLACE RETURNER

Returning to work after a significant break like long term illness, having a baby or raising a family can be a great opportunity for a coaching discussion with your staff member. Priorities often become more complicated, stress levels often increase and for some people (men and women) there can be a sense that there is somehow more to prove at work - confidence can be knocked.

Reconnecting with the world of work will be of importance where the person has been out of the workplace for a significant period, and it will be helpful to ensure that there is clarity over what has changed in the business since they originally left. Ideally, you'll have done this throughout their period away from work.

G GOAL	• Tell me about what you'd like to achieve now that you're back at work. Explore • What are the main priorities for you now? • What questions do you have about how things have changed here while you've been away? • What have been the main challenges that you have faced since returning to work? • What have you noticed as the main differences about work since you returned? • I'd like to share my thoughts on what your main deliverables at work should be, and am keen to explore what you think of my ideas.
R REALITY	• How does your work currently compare to what you'd like to achieve? • To what extent have you been able to make those your priorities so far? • What's been getting in the way of a successful return to work for you? • When was the last time that you felt like that at work (confident/in control/achieving etc.)? • How do my ideas for your responsibilities at work compare with what you'd like to achieve? • How is that missing knowledge impacting your ability to deliver at work? • How do you feel about your career right now? • How are/is your hours/skills/responsibilities/workload impacting your return to work?
O OPTIONS	• What ideas do you have about where to go for information? • Who do you know that's already successfully achieved that? Explore how they might be able to share ideas and resources. • What could you do to regain that feeling of being confident/in control/achieving etc? • How would things change if the barriers were removed? Explore. • What was different about the time when you did feel confident/in control/achieving? Explore. • Are there any other opportunities in the organisation that would make it easier to achieve that? • How could you develop those skills to make your life easier?
W WILL	• When could that realistically be achieved? • What could be the first step that you take towards making that happen? • What will have changed when you've achieved it? • What are you committed to do to make that happen? • What might get in the way? How will you overcome it? • To what extent will this address your overall goal? • What support would you like from me?

PRESENTATION SKILLS COACHING

It's been said that speaking in front of other people ranks as highly as dying in some people's list of fears…so if you have a member of your team that isn't 100% confident about a presentation they need to deliver, you might consider having a coaching discussion with them to help them prepare and grow their confidence.

G **GOAL**	• What are the key messages that you would like your audience to take from your presentation? Are you trying to reach a decision? Persuade people to act? Share information, expertise or results? Do you want to win business? • What do you want the people in the audience to think/feel/believe/understand about your presentation? How do you want them to react? • What do you know about the people who are going to be in the audience? How do they prefer to receive information? What is their likely level of existing knowledge about your presentation materials? • How long do you want your presentation to last? What is on the agenda before/after your presentation
R **REALITY**	• What obstacles are you likely to face during your presentation? • What information is currently included in your presentation? To what extent will this information convey your key messages? • When have you successfully persuaded people to take action/reach a decision/offer business before? • What feedback have you previously had about your presentation skills? • What questions are likely to come up during the presentation? • With the current materials, how long does your presentation last? How do you know this? • How are YOU feeling about the presentation that you are going to deliver? • What impact is the agenda before/after your presentation likely to have? • What are the areas that are likely to give you the most trouble with delivering? • How is your audience likely to respond to your presentation?
O **OPTIONS**	• What ideas do you have for overcoming these obstacles? • What other presentations or discussions have you delivered before? How did they go? • What have you learned because of doing other presentations before now? • Where could you go to research the content? • Who might have delivered a similar sort of information before? What could you learn from them? • How could you get feedback from this presentation so that you can improve even more next time? • What could you do if things don't go to plan during the presentation? • Who could you practice with for feedback? • How could you ensure that what you present will resonate with all attendees? How could you tailor your presentation to respond to learning styles? • How have you dealt with your nerves in other situations? What has worked for you before?
W **WILL**	• What are the logistics for ensuring you have everything you need? What will you wear? What other resources do you need? • Who else needs to/could be involved in designing the presentation content? • Are there any other people that need to be there? Who? • What is the first thing you need to do? What order do things need to occur? • What action is required to ensure that the possible obstacles are overcome before your presentation? • When are you planning to achieve that? • What support do you need from me?

COACHING A SENSITIVE PERSONAL ISSUE

We've all experienced the person in our team who we KNOW we need to say something to, but we're just not sure where to start. Maybe they always talk loudly – disturbing the rest of the team, perhaps they constantly interrupt others, or they always believe they are right. Perhaps they dress inappropriately, are always negative or their rudeness is preventing their advancement.

While coaching is not always the answer (sometimes you will find that a more direct, performance intervention is required – refer to the **Coaching Continuum Model**), using the sort of questions below might just help you to deal with things before they get out of hand. The difference with this conversation may be that you are the one driving the goal and the actions to begin with, particularly if the employee has a low level of self-awareness of the impact they are having.

Using a robust feedback model and exploring some resources that are focussed on Emotional Intelligence might also be helpful with this sort of conversation. Seek support from your HR team if you are unsure or worried.

G GOAL	• I've noticed that when you ABC (insert observable behaviour) the result is that XYZ (insert a tangible result) • I'd like to support the development of your career in the business here and to do that we need to work together to address a couple of things...specify. • I need to have a difficult conversation with you – I'm really sorry to have to do it but it's important that we get this into the open now and I begin to help you tackle it. • I want to start by apologising that nobody has talked to you about ABC until today. • I'd like to understand more about what causes you to be so ABC (insert observable behaviour).
R REALITY	• What impact do you think that ABC (insert observable behaviour) has on the other people in the team? • How might that ABC (insert observable behaviour) be perceived by others? • What impact might that ABC (insert observable behaviour) have on your career or your success at work? • What do you think lies behind your decision to behave in ABC (insert observable behaviour) manner? What causes you to be like ABC (insert observable behaviour)? • What prevents you from behaving more like (insert opposite behaviour to ABC)? • How would you prefer people to describe you in the office?
O OPTIONS	• What different ways could you achieve the same end goal, but perhaps without doing ABC? • In the future, what else could you do or say to be more like the person you would like to be? • Has there ever been a time when you were less ABC (insert observable behaviour)? Explore. • I'd like to share some thoughts that I have for things that could be changed, and then we'll work out together what we're going to do together to achieve them.
W WILL	• I'm committed to helping you to make a change, what can I do to help you get you started? • How about you summarise back to me what we've talked about just now, and then we'll agree together what we're going to do to address it. • What can I do to help you become more (or less) ABC (insert observable behaviour)? • I would like us to achieve this change to ABC (insert observable behaviour) by DATE, how often would you like us to review your progress to achieve this? • If things don't change, one of the consequences might be (insert consequences) so I'd really like to avoid that. Let's agree right now what we're going to do to prevent that from happening.

COACHING TO EMBED LEARNING

Teaching your employees new skills is one thing...getting them to apply what they have just learned is another – and that means potentially hundreds (or thousands) of dollars wasted.

A common outcome is for delegates to leave a training intervention all fired up and ready to make exceptional changes to the way that they work – only for their day job to get in the way when they return to the office. Coaching can help to reflect on the learning that has taken place, and ensure that a commitment is made to bring some of the learning back to work – whether the result of a conference, training workshop or reading a development book.

A recommendation would be to have this discussion within 10 days of the training intervention, and to repeat the discussion after 12 weeks and 6 months to understand how new skills/knowledge/capabilities are being embedded.

G GOAL	• When you signed up to do (insert training intervention) what was the main purpose of doing so? • When you decided to do (insert training intervention) what was the main driving force for choosing it? • What were some of the key things that you have learned because of (insert training intervention)? • If you had to summarise the main benefits that you have taken from attending (insert training intervention) what would they be? • Part of the reason that you attended the (insert training intervention) was to have a positive impact on (insert skill/knowledge/capability) because of feedback (possibly from 360 or performance review) – let's look at what you've learned together. • When was the last time that you attended a training programme and made significant (and positive) changes to how you work as a result?
R REALITY	• When we look at how you currently perform using (insert skill/knowledge/capability), what would you say are some of the main differences compared with what you've learned during the training intervention? • Think about somebody in our organisation, or somebody that you know that already uses this new knowledge/skills/capability and is regarded as exceptional. What do you notice about how they do things differently? How might they be able to help or mentor you? • What was it about the training programme that resulted in significant (and positive) changes which encouraged you or enabled you to change the way that you work? How could we use this information to ensure that you can make the same positive changes this time?
O OPTIONS	• What different options are there for you to adapt the way that you use the knowledge/skills/capabilities you've learned on the (insert training intervention) at work? • It sounds as though some things may be preventing you from being able to make the changes that you've learned during the training intervention. What ideas do you have for ways that we could work together to overcome these obstacles? • What ideas do you have because of taking part in (insert training intervention) that might be of particular benefit to our team/our organisation? • What lessons can you learn from changes that you have made previously because of attending training interventions? How might you apply them in these circumstances?
W WILL	• How are we going to measure the results/success of the changes that you are committing to make because of the training? • What specifically are you committing to change because of attending the training intervention? • What support do you need from me to be able to make the required changes to your knowledge/skills/ capability as a result of the discussion we have had today? • When shall we get together again to talk about the changes that you have made because of the training, and the impact those changes are having on you at work? • As your manager, what can I do more of/less of to improve the embedding of the learning you have invested in doing?

COACHING TO EXPLORE SALES OUTCOMES

Sales conversations are critical to pretty much every organisation – whether you are selling a widget, a product or a service, success in this area can often meant the difference between a successful business – and a disastrous one.

A coaching discussion to debrief a sales meeting or sales conversation can bring valuable learning to your team members, in addition to giving you the opportunity to encourage them to grow their capabilities and achieve more for your company. You may also decide to observe your team during their sales calls and include some of these questions to provide a structure to debrief what you see.

G GOAL	• When you originally booked the meeting/made the call with your client – what was the main outcome that you were looking for? • During the sales meeting/call with your client, what was the overall outcome that you understood your client to be looking for? • Can you think of the last really positive/successful sales meeting/call that you had - when you reached a really great outcome with a client? • How much time do you typically spend on a sales call/meeting with a client where the outcome is successful? What do you do to prepare?
R REALITY	• To what extent did you meet the outcomes you were hoping to achieve? Or that your client was hoping to achieve? • What was it about the really positive/successful sales meeting/call that you did differently? • What client objections did you experience during the call – and to what extent had you prepared for them? What solutions did you present to objections and how successful were they? • What questions did you ask to understand fully the needs and requirements of the client during the sales meeting/call? • What got in the way of reaching an agreement with the client during the sales meeting/call? • Even though the sales meeting/call did not go as planned what have you learned about your client? How can you use this knowledge to help you in the future? • What went really well in the sales meeting/call? What could have gone better? Was there anything that surprised or concerned you during the meeting?
O OPTIONS	• What could you have said or done in order to lead your client in different directions during the sales meeting/call in order to get a different outcome? • What ideas do you have for things you could do differently next time to improve the outcome of the sales meeting/call? • What different options or solutions could you have suggested to the client because of your knowledge of the products and services that we offer in our company? How could you find out more information about the products and services that we offer to better help your client next time? • What ideas do you have for how you will plan the conversation differently next time to achieve a different outcome? • What were all the different tools and methods that you used during the sales meeting/call? Which ones were the most successful?
W WILL	• How are we going to measure the success of the changes you plan to make to your sales meetings/calls as a result of this conversation? • What are the main changes that you are going to commit to making because of the conversation we have had today? • Thinking of the ideas you've had today, what are the new ideas or approaches that you're going to take with your client? • When are we going to get back together to discuss the impact of the changes on your sales results? • What will be the impact of making some of the changes we have discussed to your overall sales targets or appointments? • What support do you need from me?

Coaching to GROW HR Business Partner Skills (designed to support an HR Conference)

It's a widely cited fact that people are a key driver of business results. It's also generally expected that the Human Resources team are the people professionals, with a deep understanding of their workforce – but is HR doing enough with that knowledge to drive business outcomes?

Stepping into a proactive HR Business Partner (HRBP) role can require different skills compared with those of more traditional HR delivery. Use the Conversation Guide below to consider how you might play an even stronger role in supporting the direction of HR in your business.

*This Conversation Guide was inspired by the content of the Human Capital Institute Whitepaper, 2014 "The Decade of HR" and the Deloitte's 2015 survey "Human Capital Trends".

G GOAL	• How would you describe the Knowledge, Skills and Experience required to be an amazing HRBP in your business? (e.g. using the HRBP Skills Assessor on page 2). Consider using Job Descriptions or PD's from another business. • According to the HCI Whitepaper, the goal of the HRBP is to "improve the workplace and workforce so that the business unit executes its strategy and is successful" – how are you currently contributing to this in your business? What are your main areas of focus? • What data would help your business to be more effective? Where are their biggest people issues and how could you make those issues go away? (Tip: who have you asked in senior leadership? What trends have you observed? ☺)
R REALITY	• How would you benchmark your existing HRBP Knowledge, Skills and Experience? (consider asking for feedback?). Prioritize where your opportunities lie. • Keep a diary for one week - describe the challenges that your stakeholders ask you to resolve. Are you solving operational problems (e.g. producing data on headcount, absence, supporting grievances etc.) or being invited to more strategic and predictive discussions? Consider using the HRBP Skills Assessor to track where you spend your time. • To what extent do you provide advice and answers for your business vs asking coaching questions to grow business capability, understanding and ownership of outcomes? • What People Analytics do you currently use (beyond headcount and retention rates…e.g. ideas below). Where are your opportunities? • How do you already measure your core HR activities (e.g. who are the interviewers with the highest rate of successful candidates? Where are your worst absence levels and why?)
O OPTIONS	• What is your preferred learning style? How can you use this knowledge to choose development which builds your HRBP capability? • How can you use knowledge gained from other learning events (e.g. HRBP Conference) to develop your Knowledge, Skills and Experience (who did you meet? What did you learn? How are you using this to your advantage?) • What do other companies in your industry do to track People Analytics (e.g. their tools, resources, software e.g. EnableHR). How well do they work? • What ideas for HRBP best practice can you find from leading companies? (Tip: look at Kenexa Best Workplaces, Glassdoor.com, Deloitte Top 200?) • How can you learn more about the capability of your existing People Analytics tools? • Who are your key HRBP stakeholders and how can you find out more about what's important to them? • How could you keep up to date with the key trends, challenges and opportunities within your industry in New Zealand and overseas? • How will you know when you are successfully operating as an HRBP? What differences will you see? What differences will your business see?

W WILL	• Using the results of your HRBP Skills Assessor - what are you going to do immediately to increase your HRBP skills? • What would a quick fix for your business challenges look like? What would it take to create a "better" solution? E.g. trending data over time, comparing software options? • What are you going to do in the next 12 months to increase your HRBP skills? • How can you build your professional profile as an HRBP within your business (e.g. who needs to know your focus and your achievements? Who could champion you?) • Who can help you to develop your Knowledge, Skills and Experience – perhaps other business areas or industry leaders to collaborate with? (Tip: talk to IT, Comms, Health & Safety, Quality and/or Finance?)

HRBP Skills Assessor - The following framework has been adapted from the Human Capital Institute Whitepaper 2014. It identifies the most desirable skills for an effective HRBP.

For each HRBP Skill listed, give yourself a score between 1 (no skills) and 10 (perfectly skilled). Use the results to prioritize your action plan for professional development and/or focus in order to build your HRBP skills.

Choose up to three Skills that you are passionate about and explore how they might bring business benefits by discussing with stakeholders – then focus on becoming confident in those skills…and driving change. Remember to measure and report your results.

Understanding the Business	Leveraging Talent	Consult & Implement Change
• Business Acumen • Financial Literacy • Analyse People Analytics • Data driven decisions	• Business impact of Talent practices • Building Trust • Strengthen engagement, collaboration & retention	• Consulting skills • Coaching Skills • Influencing skills • Understand perspective of business leaders • Understanding Change

People Analytics - Some ideas for what you could consider tracking, monitoring and/or understanding. Remember that other teams may already be tracking this data (not necessarily HR).

Look for business analytic support to help you interpret data, and make recommendations to your business for areas they could focus on.

Recruiting & Workforce Planning
- Identifying and hiring successful employees (e.g. linking to high/medium/low performers)
- Tracking and improving diversity data
- Predicting the success of hiring decisions

Compensation & Benefits
- Understanding the impact of Pay Policies (e.g. what impact on high/medium/low performers?)
- Exploring the likely impact of innovative approaches in other organisations or industries

Performance, Succession,
- Revenue generation (e.g. calculating the value of high performers compared with medium)
- Mapping high performing attributes and characteristics back to the recruitment process

Learning & Leadership
- Measuring Leadership skills and tracking how they influence individual/team performance
- 360 reviews linked with coaching programmes for tailored professional development
- Measuring the success of learning initiatives - including job rotations, self directed etc.

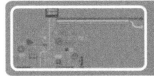

Employee Data
- Correlating HR data to business performance - what do your star employees "look like"?
- Profiling/forecasting employees who may be a Health & Safety risk

Engagement & Retention
- Prediciting retention - including retention algorithms
- Tracking the impact of wellness initiatives
- Measuring and driving collaboration

GROW Your Coaching Culture (designed for a company training internal coaches)

Over the last decade (and counting!) coaching as a tool for leaders and managers has become renowned as a driver for many desirable outcomes in business.

Professional accountability, improved work performance, better time management, increased team effectiveness, enriched relationships, greater self-confidence, enhanced communication skills…and even a positive impact on business management. These are all quoted benefits of using a coaching approach at work according to an ICF study in collaboration with PriceWaterhouse Coopers 2013.

Harvard Business Review's Pocket Mentor Series built on these suggestions by including even more business focused outcomes like: overcoming costly business issues (using the solution focus of coaching), strengthening employee's skills so they can grow at work (and therefore potentially step into your leadership shoes), improved retention and reducing the cost of training.

Wouldn't it be great to know that the investment that YOUR business is making into developing a coaching culture can be tracked – so you can understand the impact of any coaching related initiatives?

Either use the questions below to support your own reflective thinking about Coaching in your workplace, or consider how they might benefit a more general discussion about coaching with your leadership team.

G Goal	• What is the overall driver for growing a coaching culture at YOUR workplace? • How will you know when you have a coaching culture? What will you see/hear/do/experience that's different? • How will your customers or stakeholders benefit from coaching? • How will your employees benefit from coaching? • How will the managers and leaders benefit from coaching? • What are the key conversations where you'd like more coaching to take place (e.g. at specific meetings? In career discussions? Resolving issues? Post project reviews?) • Are there specific groups that you'd like to target for coaching? (e.g. maternity returners? New managers?)
R Reality	• Right now, what are the conversations like at work? (e.g. directive vs coaching in style) • How would you describe the health of the culture you're hoping to influence (e.g. solution focused teams? Problem focused teams? Dependent on management?) • What do you already measure that might change as a result of introducing a coaching culture (e.g. engagement survey? Turnover? Absence? Career planning?) • What is likely to get in the way of growing a coaching culture at your workplace? • What will cause resistance from stakeholders? Employees? Managers & leaders? • What has been the experience of coaching in other parts of your business/industry – and how could you access their learning? • What is the problem that you are hoping a coaching culture will help you to solve?

O Options	• What ideas do you have for highlighting the successes of coaching? (e.g. newsletters, profiles, role models) • What new metrics could you begin tracking right now so you can understand the impact that a coaching culture has on them (e.g. absence, turnover, retention, 360 of managers & leaders who are going to coach) • What does research suggest is the evidence are you likely to see because of coaching at work? (e.g. improved engagement within specific teams? Reduced absence? More internal promotions/applications for promotion?) • How could you reward coaching at work so that it is a desirable skill or behaviour? • What could be implemented to support groups of managers and leaders who coach? (e.g. peer coaching forums, external executive coaching, coaching "buddies", coaching qualifications) • What are alternative ways of solving the problem you want coaching to solve? • What do other companies do to track the success of coaching at work?
W Will	• What are the quick measures of success that you can implement right now to understand the impact of coaching at work? • What will you need to design or implement over the next 12-24 months? (or longer) • What will you do to ensure that your coaching culture is directly linked to the vision and/or strategies of your company? • Who are the other stakeholders of coaching that could support you in understanding, measuring and championing the impact of a coaching culture? • What will you do to measure the specific impact of coaching on employees? • How often are you going to take a snapshot of the impact of a coaching culture to ensure that it becomes embedded into your business?

In addition to these questions, it could be beneficial for you to ask for more formal feedback about any executive or external coaching that you invest in for your team. Some example questions include:

1. **What positive differences have you noticed since you began your coaching programme; At work? In your team? At home?**

2. **What have been the most valuable tools and resources you have gained because of coaching? Approximately what $ value do you think that tool or resources is worth to you? How will you use the tools or resources at work?**

3. **If you could summarise one key benefit that you have experienced from coaching discussions what would it be?**

BACKWARDS COACHING

Coaching isn't just about looking forward and planning the action that you will take, it can also be about looking backwards to reflect on what you have learned and what you will do differently if the circumstances or need arises in the future.

A medical industry client uses this approach to debrief when they have issues in the hospital, particularly when "in the moment" coaching is not acceptable. Another construction industry client used this approach to create better outcomes at the end of each project.

Use these questions to do some self-reflecting or to have a conversation with your team. Adapt the questions so they fit your own circumstances.

G GOAL	• What was the overall goal when you delivered XYZ at work? • What were the key outcomes we were looking for? • What were the overall constraints that we wanted to overcome? • Who were the major competitors that we wanted to outperform? • Who were the main people we wanted to influence? • What outcomes had we committed to with our clients? • To what extent did our achievements of XYZ contribute to the overall Vision for this company? • Summarise the objectives for XYZ in one sentence.
R REALITY	• On reflection, to what extent did we meet our aims? How do we know this – feedback? • I'd like to share my own thoughts on how well we achieved against our deliverables - SHARE • How well were those outcomes achieved? • I'd like YOU to share your ideas on how well we achieved our goals. • On a scale of 1-10, how well did we influence those people/achieve those goals? What would we need to change to increase that score? • Was there anything that didn't go to plan? • What were some of the key lessons that we learned? • Were there any deadlines or milestones that we missed? What ideas do you have about why we missed them? • Summarise the three key learnings from XYZ.
O OPTIONS	• What ideas do YOU have for things we need to do to ensure that our overall aims are achieved or achieved better next time? • How could we get things back on track for the rest of our programme? • If we were doing XYZ again, from the start – what would we do differently? • What do we need to change about XYZ in the future? What else or who else could we include next time? • What are the really great things that we achieved that could be applied to XYZ in the future? How will we share them? • Are there any similar events in the organisation that might benefit from our learning?
W WILL	• What are we specifically committing to do after this review? • Who is going to take ownership of XYZ actions? • When are we going to achieve this by? • Who else needs to be involved in our plans? • What support do you need from me as the overall leader of this project? • What do we need to do right now, and what should we plan for in the future? • What ideas do we need to test in order to decide whether to progress them? How will we test them?

EVENT PLANNING

I was specifically asked to write this for an entertainment industry client.

If your role, or that of your team involves organising events or functions then self-coaching (or having a coaching discussion) can help to prepare and plan for success.

G GOAL	• Our goal is to organise world class events and competitions that highlight the breadth and depth of the ability and skills of our members – how will your event or function align to this? • What does a world class event or competition include? How will we benchmark this one? • What is the overall intent of this event or function – how will attendees engage with the primary industries at this event? • Who are you hoping will attend – who is the ideal delegate and when is a convenient time for them to attend? Age groups? Demographics? • Where do they find out information about events or functions like this (e.g. posters? Schools? Online? Direct mailing?) • What are the three critical outcomes that you are hoping for? Educating? Celebrating? Persuading? Connecting? Fund raising? Consider a career in the Primary Industry? What else? • What is the overall budget for organising this event? • How will you identify the specific details for this event or function? The venue? The catering? The attendees? The promotions and publicity? The content? Seeking feedback? Any handouts or takeaways? Sponsors? Tidying up? Parking? Technologies required? Special assistance? • Who else do you need to support you in organising this event or function? How will you stay in touch with their actions? What do they need to know from you? • What role do YOU want to play in this event or function? Organiser? Speaker? Reception welcome?
R REALITY	• What obstacles might get in the way of achieving the goals we have identified for our event or function? • When was the last time you organised a really successful world class event or function? How did you do it? • Who else in the team/organisation has organised an event like this previously? • Who are the caterers/venues/sponsors etc. that you have used previously and how successful were they? • What systems do we have access to that will help us to track our way towards a successful event or function? • What lessons have you or others in the team learned from previous events or functions like this? • How are we going to check and review what people think of our event or function – from attendees? From suppliers? From presenters?
O OPTIONS	• What ideas do you have to achieve the goals of our event or function within the budget that we have been assigned? • What other ways could we achieve the goals of our event or function but using a different means to achieve them? Get creative! • Taking each specific detail one at a time, (e.g. venue, catering, promotions) how many other ideas do you have – e.g. alternative venues, caterers, promotion means etc. • Who else do you know who might be able to provide ideas or support for this event or function? • How will you record what happened to ensure your ideas are used by others organising a similar event or function at the organisation? • If you were to run this event again, what would you change? What would you keep the same? Keep a record of your learning as you go along.
W WILL	• How will you plan and prioritise the actions that you need to take? Check-lists? Online tracking? • What might get in the way? How will you overcome it? • What support do you need, and from whom? • How can I help to ensure this event or function has a really great outcome? How can I stay in touch to check where you're at with the organising? • What will you do in the future to ensure that events or functions like this are even better?

BUSINESS REVIEW

I was asked to write the following conversation guide for a new business who wanted
to have a 12-month review of their successes.

G GOAL	• Who are your target clients – industry? Size? Location? • Describe the sort of work that you would love to be doing. Include as much detail as possible. • If you fast forward 12 months, how will you know that your business is a success? What measures will you use? How frequently will you check progress against this? How will you check that measures are balanced (not just P&L or $ focussed)? • When you started your business, what sort of work did you see yourself doing? What skills and strengths were you hoping to use? • If you summarised your business focus in one sentence, what would it be? • How do you want clients to "find" you?
R REALITY	• How would you describe your clients right now: those you've worked with over the last 12 months? • What industry are they in? size? Location? How do they currently find you? • When has work been exciting (not stressful) over the last 12 months (when you've looked at the time and realised that hours have passed you by)? What were you doing? How can you do more of this? • Same question for when things have been very stressful. Get as much detail as possible (e.g. WHY...not just "we didn't win a bid") How can you do less of this? • What are your measures currently telling you about your business success? Which bits are most successful? Least successful? • If you review all of the work you've delivered in the last 12 months, what have been the patterns or trends? What sort of client has purchased the most (pro-rated as required)? Or recommended most work to you? • What is your process for closing out work with a client and finding out what their experience has been of working with you? How does it compare with your target business vison/focus? What are the themes or trends that clients are reporting about the impact of your business? • How do you currently convey your business focus to clients? Bring it to life?
O OPTIONS	• How could you leverage the experience of the clients who work with you? Using their references and recommendations? How do other similar competitors achieve this? • How could you more efficiently target the clients you'd like to work with? • How might a customer loyalty or referral programme work for your business? • What other businesses do you know who have grown fast/in their first 2yrs – how did they do it? How do the best businesses grow fast? In your industry? In other industries? Outside New Zealand? • What ideas do you have about achieving the priorities you see in the business right now? • How else could you connect to all the business events in the region or your target industry etc. (to attend as participants and therefore create new connections with attendees?) • Who is selling a similar product/offer/service really well globally? How are they doing it?
W WILL	• What do you need to do immediately? • What are you going to plan into your annual goals? Next six months? Next 12 months? • What are the easy, high impact actions (JFDI)? Harder high impact actions (plan them)? Hard low impact actions (bin them)? easy low impact actions (check they really need doing)? • How are you going to spread the load, while playing to strengths and passions? • Who else could help you? How could they achieve this without being FT employed? Or by being FT employed? • How can you ensure that you remain agile, while staying focussed on your bigger goals? • How can you use social media to support you? Or not? • What other business development support do you think you need right now?

Solution Focussed Questions

Encouraging a focus on the positive; what is to be <u>gained</u> from change and ideas for <u>solving</u> problems will contribute greatly towards shifting energy and building engagement towards solutions. Here are a few ideas to get you started:

- Has there ever been a time when it DID work? What was different? What do we need to change?
- Do you know any employers that have a better process than we do? What is different about it?
- What ideas do you already have of things we need to do differently in order to get better results?
- Has anybody else experienced this particular issue? What have you tried to do to resolve it?
- What action have we already taken? What is working and what else could we do?
- Despite some of these issues, what is going really well?
- What changes have you noticed since this issue was first identified? How are things improving?
- What lessons have we learned from things going wrong previously? How can we apply those lessons in this situation?
- What ideas do you have about things we need to overcome?
- It's never worked? Never EVER? (to challenge general statements that change won't work)
- Can you think of a company/industry/person who might have overcome this before us? How could we learn from them?
- What would we like to leave behind from this situation? What will we carry forward and take with us?
- On a scale of 1-10, what would we give this particular issue? What would need to change for it to be a 9 or a 10 out of 10?
- What's the smallest sign we can look for that things are improving?

The " miracle question"

- If you had all the money in the world, what would you do?
- If I could wave a magic wand and make all the problems disappear how would it be different?
- If you did know the answer what would it be?
- Suppose we were doing things exactly the way that we want...how would things be different? What would people say about us?
- If you knew there was no way that you could fail, what would you do?
- How would Superman/Spiderman/other appropriate super hero deal with this?
- If I wasn't here, what would you do?
- What might be the first thing you did? And the next?

ONE MINUTE COACHING QUESTIONS

One of the most common challenges to coaching that is highlighted by managers and leaders alike is that there isn't enough time for coaching discussions.

Yet all too often there are glimmers of coaching opportunities that crop up when you least expect them for example; bumping into a colleague at the coffee shop who's trying to decide about a project, spotting a team member who's still sitting at their desk late into the evening, overhearing a discussion between two colleagues where one is clearly unhappy in their role.

Each of these offers the chance for a quick discussion which could result in empowering the other person to review their options and decide to act. Here are a few ideas for questions that you could throw into the conversation, try them and see what happens.

G GOAL	• What do you want to accomplish? • What are you trying to do? • What is it specifically that you're trying to achieve overall? • How do you know this goal is worth achieving? • How will you (or I) know when you have achieved it? • What do you wish it was like instead?
R REALITY	• How does your current circumstance compare with what you're trying to achieve? • What's stopping you from achieving your goal? • What is it like today? • What's getting in the way? • What have you already done towards achieving your goal? What worked or didn't work? • Have you ever had to solve something like this before? What did you do? • What's happening right now?
O OPTIONS	• What are the different paths or options that you could consider? • What have you already tried? Explore. • Have you ever been in the situation before? Explore. • What alternatives do you have now? • What are the possibilities in front of you? • Which choices do you have at this time? • What have you seen work in similar situations? • If constraints were removed what would you do? • What else do you need to consider? • Who might be able to help?
W WILL	• Which of these paths or options will give you the most likely chance of achieving your overall goal? • What do you need to do next? • What can you do now? • What are your next steps? • What will it cost you if you don't take action? • What might get in the way? • Who needs to know? • What support do you need and from whom? • What will it take to get moving towards your goal?

GREAT COACHING QUESTIONS

By now I hope you've seen some coaching questions that give you inspiration to create your own.

Use this next section as a planning tool for your own Essential Conversations at work, noting your favourites.

 I've included some more great coaching questions to help you out further which are frequently used in coaching discussions…feel free to adapt them to your own personal style.

Using questions that begin with "what, where, how, who, when" are most likely to drive an open discussion, and avoid asking "why" because it can sometimes accidentally close down discussions, unless you are already a confident coach.

There are also frameworks at the end of this section to help you to plan your own coaching discussions.

- How else might that be interpreted?
- How could that fit with your overall goal/vision?
- What will be different when you've achieved that?
- If nothing changes, what might be the outcome?
- If you did know the answer, what might it be?
- Imagine you do know…now what do you think/do/say?
- What if that wasn't the case?
- What happens if you do that? What happens if you don't do that? What doesn't happen if you do that? What doesn't happen if you don't do that?
- If you knew there was no way you could fail what would you do?
- Whose voice is telling you that?
- What are you learning from the situation right now?
- Put yourself in the other person's shoes…what might they think/experience/do?
- What decisions have you avoided so far?
- Is that something that you know, or something that you believe/assume?
- What is pulling you to do that? What is pushing you to achieve that?
- What are you ready to commit to?
- How will work be different when you achieve that?
- What is it that you don't want to hear from others?
- So, what's your gut feel about this?
- Has there ever been a time when you've faced something similar? What happened? What did you do?
- What has stopped you so far? What's preventing you from taking action?
- What are you going to do differently this time?
- What else? Anything else?
- How would another person (possibly a mentor or an inspirational person) deal with the situation?
- What are the risks of succeeding (or achieving that?)

*For even more awesome questions please read; Megginson, D & Clutterbuck, D (2004) Techniques for Coaching and Mentoring; Butterworth Heinemann, Oxford

DISCUSSION OVERVIEW	G
	R
	O
	W

DISCUSSION OVERVIEW	G
	R
	O
	W

DISCUSSION OVERVIEW	G
	R
	O
	W

DISCUSSION OVERVIEW	G
	R
	O
	W

CHRISTCHURCH EARTHQUAKE – COACHING IN TRAUMATIC EXPERIENCES

In September 2010, the lives of all those who live in and around Christchurch were changed beyond belief.

On September 4th at 4:36am a substantial earthquake measuring 7.1 on the Richter scale rocked the region, and then on February 22nd, 2011 a shallower but more violent quake brought a heart-breaking number of deaths and far more serious destruction and disruption to the city.

For businesses, the result of these quakes was to a large degree absolute chaos - with many offices requiring relocation and many business owners facing painful decisions about the future viability of their products and services. Suddenly managers and leaders were required not only to help their team continue delivering against business requirements, but also operate in a working environment that saw over 2,500 large aftershocks within an eight-week period.

For employees, there was a serious impact on both an emotional and practical scale. Uncertainty over the structural reliability of homes and anxiety as a result of a relentless stream of aftershocks was compounded by insecurity over the long-term future of work as many businesses were forced to close or relocate from the region.

From a personal perspective, our home in Brooklands was damaged beyond repair in the first quake, and my CBD office was officially written off in July 2011 because of the extensive damage to the building. My husband and I literally had to walk away from the world we had created together – but we were both alive.

Working from an assortment of cafes around the city I continued my coaching, and I also used the opportunity to explore how coaching techniques and positive psychology can play an important part in personal rebuild following a traumatic event like this. I am currently writing a book about these experiences, which will be published by Routledge in 2017.

During this time, I was also asked to provide a coaching tool to support some of the managers and leaders I worked with and as a result, I've included this section within this book. If you are required to lead a team through a major disaster I sincerely hope that these coaching questions help you.

I would like to use this opportunity to formally thank all the amazing people who were responsible for rebuilding Christchurch during this time.

The infrastructure and main facilities like power, water etc. are for the most part reinstated within hours or days of major aftershocks, and contractors, council workers and other related industries work tirelessly – often around the clock - to get the city back up and running.

They are all an absolute credit to New Zealand and make me even prouder to live here.

Personal Review – Christchurch Earthquakes

Trauma is a central part of the human experience. One formal definition of a traumatic event is; …*any event that can be considered to be outside of the individuals usual experience and which has the potential to cause physical, emotional or psychological harm.*

Different people respond to traumatic events in different ways. Many of us can experience distress – emotional and physical – in the immediate days and weeks afterwards.   However, some individuals can find themselves more profoundly impacted – either the distress doesn't get any better, gets worse over time or it resurfaces unexpectedly. Either way, it can be a confusing and sometimes distressing experience.

Regardless of how you have experienced the earthquakes, it can be helpful to take a few moments to reflect on what happened so that if you ever face similar circumstances in the future you are even better resourced and feel more prepared. Use the following questions (or modify them so that you can work with your team to complete a review…you might even decide to complete this review with your family).

The questions below should not replace professional counseling and I would recommend that if your company provides access to formal psycho-social support programmes, you encourage your team to use them, no matter how well they believe they are coping with things. Of course, there is also benefit to you accessing this support yourself – if you have a robust coping strategy of your own then you are in a much more powerful position to be able to help to support your team.

G GOAL	<ul><li>What was your existing plan for coping with a natural disaster like the earthquake?</li><li>How were you hoping that things would work out, if the worst ever happened?</li><li>What was your team's understanding of the action that they should take in an emergency like this?</li><li>What did you think were the main things that were going to cause you concern, or lead to issues following a natural disaster like this?</li></ul>
R REALITY	<ul><li>How did you – or your team actually react or respond when the earthquake struck?</li><li>What did you do during the first few days after the earthquake?</li><li>What were the main emotions or feelings that you - or your team - experienced?</li><li>What went really well in the first few days of the earthquake?</li><li>What do you think could have gone even better?</li><li>What do you wish you had done differently?</li><li>What had you already prepared for which came in the most useful?</li><li>What caused (or is causing) you – or your team - the most concern since the earthquake?</li></ul>
O OPTIONS	<ul><li>On reflection, how would you have liked to react or respond differently when the earthquake struck?</li><li>How would you have preferred that your team reacted or responded?</li><li>What could you have done differently in the first few days since the earthquake?</li><li>With the benefit of hindsight, how prepared do you think you were for the earthquake?</li><li>What lessons have you learned as a result of the earthquake?</li><li>What would you do differently next time?</li><li>What changes would you like to make to your emergency plans? *Visit www.getthru.govt.nz for some ideas*</li><li>Where else could you go for information that will help you to ensure that you are even better prepared next time?</li><li>If you could do one thing to reduce your level of concern, right now what could it be?</li></ul>

W WILL	<ul><li>Looking at what you would do differently next time, is there any action that you need to take right now to ensure that things are different if this happens again?</li><li>Who is going to be responsible for making those changes?</li><li>Are there any changes that you need to plan for in the longer term?</li><li>Is there anybody that needs to be involved in helping you to make that change?</li><li>When will we check back to review the changes that you have made to ensure that you will cope even better next time?</li><li>How can I support you the best right now?</li></ul>

Positive Focus

I have had the fortune to work with some incredible people since the September earthquake.

Delivering a project for St John in the immediate aftermath meant that I was exposed to working with teams completely dedicated to supporting the health and wellbeing of others. These amazing people constantly inspired with me their tireless energy and focus on others – though they also simultaneously reminded me of the importance of refueling to ensure that personal energy is sustainable, and coaching leaders through this proved to be invaluable to them.

I have worked alongside people who lost friends, loved ones and partners in the February quake – yet they continue to focus on the wellbeing of their teams, the success of their business and the safety of their families. They serve as a constant reminder to me that there is much to be grateful for in life, and I remain in awe of their strength and resilience.

Encouraging a focus on the positive – what has been gained – in addition to reflecting honestly upon loss can be hugely beneficial during times of trauma such as that experienced in Christchurch and the surrounding regions.

Here are some questions which were developed with the psychosocial team I worked with:

- How have things changed for the better since the earthquake?

- What positive differences have you noticed since the earthquake; at home? At work? In your team?

- How might things be different and better in the future because of these positive differences?

- What changes have you noticed to give you hope at work? At home? In your team?

- What new opportunities can you see for yourself? Your family? Your business?

- If you could share one thing that you are most grateful for that's come from this experience, what would it be?

CHAPTER TWO GROW YOUR TEAM

COACHING IS **EVERYWHERE**

Although coaching as a concept has arguably been around for many years (in fact, it's often quoted that Socrates was one of the original coaches – and he lived around 450 years BC!), it seems that really since the mid 2000's that the concept of applying coaching principals at work have really taken off globally.

Coaching professionals are also everywhere.

Many of them have trained formally through the numerous global coaching schools and universities that have been created to support their growth. Most of them belong to a professionally recognised body that guides their ethical practice and protects their clients. All of them have exceptional real-life experiences that provide support and inspiration for their client base.

I'm one of those coaches.

I trained with the Oxford School of Coaching & Mentoring in 2006 (www.theocm.co.uk); a career decision that built on over 15 years of experience working across a variety of Human Resources, Consulting and Management roles.

I had worked in the corporate and financial world for most of those 15 corporate years; building my own knowledge of what it's like to work with a team, and helping other managers to grow and develop the skills to manage their people.

I have designed and implemented career frameworks, led a Scottish recruitment practice, supported the development of an employee engagement model, taught feedback skills and facilitated the experiences of other managers to help them have more meaningful and 'real' conversations at work.

Since immigrating to New Zealand in 2006, I launched my own private coaching practice, where I help people to achieve their own career goals, and I use tools and resources like those presented in these books with leaders and managers to enable them to have the same sort of development discussions with their team.

While designing a series of two-day coaching workshops for managers, I realised that if I created a resource like this, I would be able to provide an extra resource for leaders and managers anywhere in the world to practically explore how coaching conversations might look and feel.

> **I hope this information helps to set the context for these books and gives you confidence in my capability to create a resource about this subject.**

The importance of sharing.

Sharing knowledge and resources is a personal passion of mine.

Keep Your Cool

My first 'real book' was published in 2009 by Penguin Random House to provide support for people who lost their job due to redundancy and pulled together my own personal experience of redundancy with my skills and experience in recruitment and HR consulting.

Going through the experience of writing and publishing that first book reminded me of the responsibility that comes with knowledge and experience – and my wish to find as many ways as possible to share what might be helpful to other people.

To support the launch of my 'real' book in 2009, I talked on the radio, appeared on TV and wrote in national (and international) media to try to provide support to as many people as possible who were facing job loss.

I wasn't paid for any of the work that I did to support my book launch, I simply wanted to share the information I had learned while researching and writing it in the hope that it could support others.

> I have just completed my second "real" book which will be published by Routledge in 2017/2018. It is a book which explores how the lessons learned from the Christchurch earthquakes about building resilience in business can be applied to growing resilience at work. Working with a team of academic researchers to understand what they learned about growing stronger in the face of adversity greatly inspired the book.

The book you're currently reading a result of what I have learned about having better coaching conversations at work. It's based on talking to hundreds of managers and leaders, about their desire to have better coaching conversations at work, and their request for a resource which gives them an idea about how to start them.

I genuinely do hope that it provides you with information to try new conversations with your team, to create new ways of motivating others and to inspire you into using the models – go on, give them a try and see what happens!

CORE COACHING SKILLS

"In an encounter with a good coach, you walk away impressed with the coach; in an encounter with a great coach, you walk away impressed with yourself".

Awesome quote, but unknown source – please contact me if it was you so I can fully acknowledge you!

Having the skills for great coaching discussions at work can be very different to the skills typically used in the 'command and control' approach that is often relied upon by leaders around the world.

- Listening to a challenge that a member of your team is facing and then offering a solution for them to try is not coaching.
- Encouraging a member of your team to develop their skills by attending a course that you recently enjoyed is not coaching.
- Setting deadlines for your team and then asking for regular updates on progress is not coaching.

"At its simplest, coaching is a conversation where the employee talks and the manager listens and asks questions...

...the conversation helps the employee to think and to decide to take action, in ways that might not have occurred to them if the conversation had not taken place".

Sir John Whitmore

If you were to search the internet for a comprehensive list of the core skills required to have a coaching conversation you would be there for HOURS!

Every school of coaching has done countless hours of research into the personal attributes that make a coaching conversation successful, and I've included links to many of their websites in the **Resources Section** of this book so that you can find out more, and decide what works for you.

We all possess these skills to a greater or lesser extent, and we can all act to develop them if necessary so that we can become even better at coaching our team, or the individuals in our team to success. Of course, we must choose to do this though.

From the work that I've done, I believe that the skills to be a good coach at work are the following seven key areas;

1. **Listening** – the ability to TRULY listen to what somebody else is telling you. No background interference from your inner voice telling you what you think the other person should do!

2. **Flexibility** – the ability to change how you work with somebody based on their natural learning style, their capabilities or their need for information. Not just applying a 'one size fits all' approach and sharing what you've tried before so the other person can copy what worked for you. And being open to changing the route that you take with them as they journey towards their work goals.

3. **Questioning** – your talent for having a good (or a great) question to help other people find their own answer, sticking with the conversation until somebody works something out for themselves or recognising when making a suggesting is appropriate.

4. **Challenging** – your confidence in having tough coaching conversations if somebody isn't achieving what they committed to, if the results aren't good enough or if the person's words and the actions just don't add up.

5. **Interest in Developing Others** – a genuine desire from you to develop all the others in your team - not just a desire to tell them what worked for you, or focus on coaching the 'easy' people. And a commitment to supporting what's right for them as well as what's right for your business, or your own team.

6. **Interest in Developing Yourself** – a genuine commitment to having a go at new skills yourself, making mistakes and learning from the experience along the way. This can be one of the hardest things about leaning into coaching skills, particularly if the approach is very different to how you normally hold conversations.

7. **Agreeing Goals** – the ability to REALLY nail what somebody is committing to achieve, by when and how it's going to be when it's achieved...in fact with coaching, sometimes all that is required is a clear goal and the rest of the requirements become obvious.

TRUST

In addition to these skills, another element that is inherent for a great coaching conversation is **Trust** – the sense that your team really believes in you; has confidence that you have their best interests at heart and knows that they can bounce ideas without judgement.

Trust is something that we earn through our words and our actions, and just like a bank account we can credit or debit our Trust account (sometimes even on a daily basis!).

If you team trusts you, they will have the confidence to share their ideas or thoughts with you in the knowledge that you won't laugh at them, or steal their thinking and call it your own. Trust will give your team members the sense that you are on their side, and they can share what they hope to achieve at work – and then you will support them.

If they don't trust you, you may need to consciously build that into your time with them first, before you even attempt to have a coaching discussion with them. Or you might need to consider offering them the opportunity to be coached by another leader if you are having major trust issues.

What other coaching skills will be important to you in your work situation?

Write them down here;

What other knowledge do you have about your leadership style which might complement your understanding of coaching? E.g. MBTI profile, DISC profile, Signature Strengths?

YOUR CORE COACHING SKILLS

"Being a good coach relies on being honest about your areas of strength and development from the start, checking your perception and then continually reviewing and building your capability".

Kathryn Jackson, careerbalance

Considering the core coaching skills required, plus the level of Trust that your team has in you as a manager, you can use this model to self-assess your own performance in the core skills for coaching.

Once you have identified the coaching skills that are your strengths or areas for development you can set yourself some goals to improve, or support other managers.

For each skill, give yourself a score out of 10 depending on how confident you would be in your capabilities. Ask yourself honestly what evidence your team, your peers or your own manager would give to support the score that you choose? Have you done any psychometric assessments (e.g. MBTI, DISC) that might support your thinking?

For example, if you've scored 9/10 for **Interest in Developing Self** then you should easily be able to write down all the personal development you've done in the last 12 months, right?

If you can't think what to write, maybe you should be honest that perhaps this isn't something you've really achieved – maybe it's more of a desire to be a 9/10!

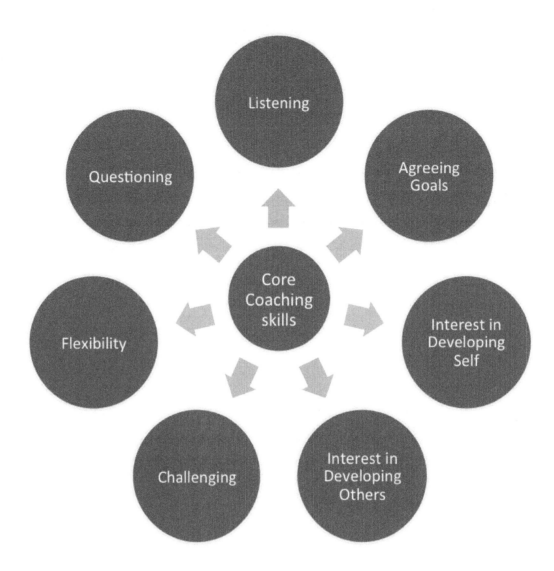

EXPLORING RESULTS

What's your highest score? This is likely to be your coaching strength.

How could you use this strength to support other managers or leaders in your business who would like to develop their coaching skills?

If it's over-extended, how might it influence your coaching? (for example, interest in "Challenging" over extended may result in you being a bit confronting with your conversations, "Questioning" over extended might result in your team being frustrated that you ask them all the time)

What's your lowest score? This is likely your coaching Achilles heel.

How might this low score impact your success in using coaching questions to GROW your team?

What ideas do you have to grow this core coaching skill?

It's very likely that not all your scores will be a perfect 10/10....so what other ideas do you have to improve your scores across the Core Skills for Coaching?

The next stage in developing a plan to improve your Core Skills for Coaching is to understand your own personal learning style.

Having a basic understanding of your personal learning style will also help you to appreciate why it is important to encourage members of your team to explore their own ideas for personal development, and not just persuade them to read a book you enjoyed, or attend a course that you found useful.

LEARNING PREFERENCES

Knowing your learning preference can help you to make better choices about how to develop your own skills, and can help you to encourage others in your team to do the same.

There are many different approaches to find out your learning style, but one that is widely used in the business is that of Honey and Mumford (1982).

The four learning styles that Honey and Mumford identified are;

1. **Activist** (DO)
     a. Immerse themselves into new experiences
     b. Tend to act first, consequences later
     c. Open minded, flexible, enthusiastic
     d. Centre of attention
     e. Likely to be enthusiastic volunteers for role plays

2. **Reflector** (REVIEW)
     a. Like to stand back and observe
     b. Collect and analyse data and slower to reach conclusions
     c. Cautious, takes a back seat
     d. Uses information from past and present to contribute to immediate observations
     e. Likely to need quiet break out time during training events to consolidate learning

3. **Theorist** (CONCLUDE)
     a. Prefer to think through problems in a logical manner
     b. Value objectivity and rationality
     c. Like to place facts into coherent theories to understand them
     d. Prefer to understand through rational order of events
     e. Like theories, models and systems in structured learning events

4. **Pragmatist** (PLAN)
     a. Keen to put new ideas and theories into practice
     b. Get impatient if there's too much discussion
     c. Confident to experiment with new ideas and techniques
     d. Tend to like getting straight to the point in training
     e. Likely to want to apply learning as soon as possible

I'm sure you can work out from the summaries that if your preferred style is that of **Reflector** (Review) then there will be little point in going on a training course where you must do lots of role plays and interactions… you will HATE it!

Similarly, if you're more of an **Activist** (Do) then choosing personal learning that is purely based on academic theories and information will drive you to distraction!

Having a basic idea of how we like to learn is vital before we jump in and book a course to develop our knowledge, skills or experience.

Most of us can learn by applying any of the learning style, but we will all have a natural preference towards one or two styles. We will likely learn best if we adopt that approach, and reflect on the changes that we make.

- **Activists**; You typically enjoy learning by doing – you'll likely want to just try your ideas out as soon as possible. Activities that appeal to you are likely to include brainstorming, experimenting, role play, group discussion and problem solving. Right now, you'll probably be thinking "Let's just get started!"

- **Pragmatists**; You naturally prefer to understand how what we learn is going to work in the real world. Activities that appeal to you are likely to include case studies and thinking about the practical applications of what you learn. You'll probably be wondering "Show me the case studies that prove it"

- **Reflectors**; You like to think about what you are learning. Activities that appeal to you will likely be reading around the subject and watching others. As you go through the book, you'll be developing ideas and saying, "Give me some time to plan my approach".

- **Theorists**; You largely learn by understanding how what you are learning fits with what you already know. Activities which will appeal to you are likely to include reading around the subject and exploring models and theories. Your key question will likely be "Help me understand the principals behind this".

If you'd like to be more scientific and take the test online to find out your preferred learning style then please visit www.peterhoney.com where you can purchase the assessment in a variety of formats.

So, what do you think is your primary learning preference?

How will you use this knowledge to help develop your coaching skills?

How will you use your knowledge of learning preferences to have better conversations with your team?

DEVELOPING YOUR CORE COACHING SKILLS

Now look at the scores you've identified for your Core Coaching Skills and focus on up to three that you would like to develop and improve upon.

Make a note of them here, and identify all the different ways that you could develop those skills – whether you are an Activist or a Reflector, a Pragmatist or a Theorist.

This will not only help you to work out how you might develop your own core coaching skills, it will also give you valuable experience in brainstorming **Options** for personal development that you can help your team to apply too, because they may not have the same learning style as you.

I've included an example so you can see what I mean.

EXAMPLE	
Questioning – *I want to get better at asking powerful questions and identifying which questions will best help my team achieve their goals.*	*Activist* – *I'm going to use the questions in this workbook, and just try them out – I'll get somebody to help me role play through them. Or I might go on a training course that lets me practice with feedback.* *Reflector* – *I want to watch somebody who asks great questions, making a note of what they ask and the response they get, then create my own approach.* *Theorist* – *I'm going to read some of the books from the resources section in this workbook, and then do some internet research to build a bank of great questions. Maybe I'll also take a short online course to help me understand how to structure questions* *Pragmatist* – *I want to use the questions in this workbook right away to help me plan for real conversations that I need to have with my team next week. I'll add my own questions too.*
1	
2	
3	

SELF COACHING

You've now created some ideas about how to develop your own skills in coaching, and to enable you to build on this at the end of this book you will find a blank GROW model so that you can make a personal commitment to the action using the framework. You've done this with a reflective self-coaching approach, reflecting on your reality, your goal some options and then a commitment to what you will do.

This self-coaching approach can be helpful for when you're having coaching discussions or creating learning plans for your team.

If you're talking about learning plans, ask your team about <u>their</u> learning style and help them to ensure that any learning interventions are tailored to that personal style. This will not only save your business money by tailoring personal development, it will speed up the learning process because your team will be using an intervention that best suits them – they will enjoy the learning!

No doubt if you're an Activist or a Pragmatist you'll want to stop reading right now and just get out there and start coaching! If so, feel free to move onto the **ESSENTIAL QUESTIONS** book at this point and begin to use the questions in your discussions at work. You can always pick up with the rest of the content later if you want.

If you're a Reflector, you to source a coaching notebook (or similar) where you can record your thinking and the ideas you have for using coaching questions at work. Perhaps you will record the **ESSENTIAL QUESTIONS** that go well, or reflect on what you might do differently next time if things don't go to plan.

If your preferred learning style is Theorist then no doubt you will want to do further reading before committing to using the **ESSENTIAL QUESTIONS** book. Please refer to the References section for some great resources to develop your knowledge even further.

Our next step in this book is to develop an understanding of the GROW model so that you can use it to support coaching conversations with your team, and to ensure that the structure of the **ESSENTIAL QUESTIONS** book makes sense to you.

INTRODUCING GROW

The GROW model for coaching is globally used as an entry level framework for coaching at work. It's simple to explain, most people 'get it' very quickly and it can be adapted for both detailed conversations and quick 'water cooler coaching 'conversations at work.

There is no single person that can be attributed to designing the GROW model, but it was prolifically profiled and used within businesses during the 1980's by **Graham Alexander, Alan Fine** and **Sir John Whitmore**.

GRAHAM ALEXANDER

Graham Alexander is often quoted as 'the world's number one executive coach', having coached more CEO's in the UK than any other coach (2010)

He has authored several books and was responsible for founding Europe's largest coaching company; the **Alexander Corporation**. This is now known as Alexander: www.thealexanderpartnership.com

---

ALAN FINE

Alan is a "New York Times bestselling author, keynote speaker and performance coaching pioneer". He is widely recognised as the co-creator of the GROW Model, and now uses his InsideOut Approach to influence worldwide.

SIR JOHN WHITMORE

After career in the racing industry, Sir John Whitmore progressed into the world of sports psychology and recognised an opportunity to take the coaching principles of Sports into the world of Business. He became a pioneer for coaching, and is globally regarded as a founding father of the approach.

He became the executive chairman of **Performance Consultants International** a wonderful team of

Very sadly for his friends, his family and the coaching world, John passed away in May 2017.

The GROW coaching model was introduced in the book '**Coaching for Performance'** (ISBN 978-1857881707), a book developed by Sir John Whitmore to support managers in using the principles of coaching within a business context. It has sold millions of copies in over 23 languages.

The acronym GROW refers to;

- **GOAL** – the goal(s) that are to be achieved, either from the specific conversation or over the longer term.
- **REALITY** – to explore the real nature of the problem; what's getting in the way, what's not going to plan or perhaps why the goal is in fact the goal.
- **OPTIONS** – exploring the possible different ways that the goal could be reached.
- **WILL (or WRAP UP)** – making a specific commitment to action towards achieving the goal.

Using a coaching framework like GROW avoids a discussion going something like this;

Employee – "here's my problem"

Leader – "I'll take your problem and I'll make it my problem and I'll add it to the list of problems that I'm already dealing with and then I'll stress about your problem and all the other problems I'm working on and then once I've worked out how to solve your problem I'll tell you exactly how I want you to solve it to make sure that your problem resolved to my satisfaction before I move onto resolving my next problem"

The GROW model can be used to structure a totally different sort of conversation, which empowers both the employee and the manager, and which doesn't just result in the manager having to come up with all the solutions.

As an example, if you were to take a specific situation from the exercise in developing your **Core Coaching Skills** and plot it through the model it might look something like this;

G	**GOAL** – my goal is to increase my capability to be flexible with my team, co-creating solutions to their problems that recognise their capability and learning styles while still meeting our business deadlines.
R	**REALITY** – right now, I prefer to share what has worked for me in the past and tell them to try that. I then like them to update me on progress at our weekly meeting so that I can be certain we're on track.
O	**OPTIONS** – I could ask my team to let me know how they prefer to learn, I could ask them if they've ever successfully tackled this sort of problem in the past, I could encourage them to identify who might have tried something similar, I could help them to think through all the possible stakeholder responses, I could ask what support they would like from me, for example whether they would like an answer or to bounce ideas, I could check with them the impact it would have on business deadlines, I could ask them who else needs to get involved…
W	**WILL** – from now on, I will encourage my team to think about their own ideas for solving the problem before coming to speak with me, and encourage them to consider if they have ever solved anything similar (or know somebody who has). I will bounce ideas with them and jointly agree the action they plan to take. I will ask how frequently they would like to update me on progress to ensure that we meet our deadlines.

Try one for yourself here;

G	What are you hoping to achieve?
R	How are things going right now?
O	What different ideas do you have to change how things are right now, to get closer to what you want to achieve?
W	What are you going to do, to get closer to what you want?

GET ON THE GRID!

While working at SCIRT (Stronger Christchurch Infrastructure Rebuild Team) in Christchurch, New Zealand my coaching audience was largely one of engineering and project management backgrounds, with a self-proclaimed preference for very "Black & White" models. The GROW model didn't quite work for them so we played with the concepts and designed our own coaching framework called GRID. This stands **for Goal, Reality, Ideas and Do**. Please feel free to use this for your coaching if you prefer.

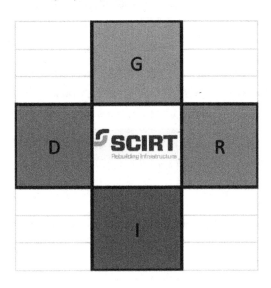

A MODEL FOR GROWING

Traditionally, the GROW model is often presented as a circular conversation that looks like this;

Using the framework in this way helps to ensure that each of the elements of the GROW model is given due attention during the conversation, and ensures that none of the steps is accidentally left out to the detriment of the outcome.

Without a **Goal,** there is little point in reviewing **Options**; without an understanding of **Reality** there can be no easy way to agree what action **Will** be taken; without agreement on what **Will** be done the **Goal** cannot be achieved…etc.

As a coach and previously as a manager I found that it wasn't always quite so easy to apply a circular model like this to 'real' discussions so I checked with other coaches and managers around the world to find out if they experienced a similar challenge.

Here are some of the main things we identified;

> People don't always arrive with a specific **Goal** that they would like to achieve…many come with their **Reality** (*"my work-life balance is all over the place and I'm losing it at work!"* or *"I've lost my job through redundancy and I'm not sure where to start"* or *"I'm going to miss an important deadline and I don't know what to do"*).

> Some people come with their **Options** (*"I've been offered a promotion at work, and I've also applied for a job outside of my employer – I'm wondering which one should I choose?"* or *"There are a number of different ways that I could tackle a problem at work and I'd like to bounce ideas with somebody"*)

> Sometimes a coaching discussion even starts with the **WILL** (*"I've just GOT to DO SOMETHING about what's going on here…",* *"I've made a decision to do something and I need your support"*)

In addition, we agreed that although some people have a clearly articulated **Goal** to start with, once they explore their **Reality** or their **Options**…their original **Goal** can sometimes change to something new, or even reshapes to reflect the new thinking that they have done.

Our thinking was that the **Goal** must be at the heart of every coaching conversation, and therefore the **GROW** model could be adapted to take this into consideration.

> In yet a further twist to our thinking on GROW, one of Europe's best known and innovative writers on the world of leadership, coaching and mentoring, David Clutterbuck suggests that having a clear articulation of the Goal may in fact become the end of the cycle – and that by helping team members to understand specifically what they need to do, the need for further coaching is negated…what do you think?

I wanted to ensure that the coaching model used in this book considers these different thoughts and scenarios–while also continuing to build on the wonderfully robust structure of the **GROW** model to support coaching conversations at work.

As a result, I got in touch with Graham Alexander directly and received his express permission to adapt the GROW model to reflect my own experience of coaching while simultaneously maintaining the integrity of the original GROW model.

I also talked to David Clutterbuck for his thinking about the information I have presented in my books, given his presence as one of coaching's leading writers and thinkers about this subject.

Because of these conversations, the GROW model we use in this book looks like this; This version of the GROW model allows for a team member to approach you with their **Reality** or their **Options**…or even their **Will** and in all cases your first step will be to guide them back to the overall **Goal** of what they are trying to achieve.

The **Goal** becomes the heart of the conversation.

This model also serves as a reminder that once a member of your team has explored their **Reality**, **Options** or **Will** you should check back with them to ensure that it will serve towards helping them achieve their overall **Goal**.

A reminder of the model will be included on each page of our **Essential Questions** so that you can easily refer to it during your conversation.

BARRIERS TO COACHING

My guess is that you're reading these books because you're going to be very committed to trying out new coaching questions and using the GROW model in your role as the manager or leader of the team.

However - let's be realistic.

Doing your job can be challenging and time consuming enough without adding something else to your 'To Do' list!

A quick search on the internet reveals that there are many 'excuses' that are often used in the business world to avoid having to coach or ask coaching questions.

These include;

- Not wanting to run the risk of making a 'mistake' or asking the 'wrong' question.
- Lack of belief in own capability to be a good coach.
- Too used to being in control and having all the answers...not comfortable with relinquishing that to others.
- Being sceptical of the impact that coaching questions will have.
- Too busy dealing with day to day issues to have a conversation with the team.
- Most comfortable with a certain type of management – "I've been doing it this way for years!"
- Not being 'close' enough to the job that the team are doing, therefore not being able to ask appropriate coaching questions.
- Not allowing enough time for coaching to have an impact and team members to act to achieve their goals.
- Worrying that giving away too much responsibility to the team too soon will result in business problems.
- Lack of somewhere to go for coaching – for example working in an open plan office.
- Can't work out when to coach and when not to coach.
- Shortage of trained or experienced coaches across the management team to ask for support.

> **What other barriers might get in the way for YOU using Essential Questions to GROW your team at work?**

KEEPING IT REAL

G	Let's assume your **GOAL** is to use coaching questions with your team…or is it something else?
R	What is your **REALITY**? Which of the issues identified above are the most likely to prevent you from coaching at work? Are there any additional challenges that you will need to overcome?
O	What ideas do you have for the different **OPTIONS** available to you in order to overcome the challenges that you have identified? Who else could help you to consider the actions you could take?
W	What **WILL** you commit to doing to achieve your goal of using coaching questions with your team?

RECAP

In reading both chapters, you have been introduced to some of the fundamental concepts of coaching at work to enable you to use great coaching questions to GROW your team;

- We've introduced coaching as an additional tool for leaders and reviewed some of the basic principles on which it's based.

- We've explored some of the core skills for coaching, and you've analysed how your own skills stack up against them.

- You've identified your likely learning style, and created some ideas for how you might improve your coaching skills.

- You have also (hopefully!) worked out the importance of having this sort of learning style knowledge about your team to help you support their personal development plans – maybe you can guess the learning style of your team members, or even better, encourage them to identify their own.

- The framework for the GROW coaching model has been introduced, and you've practiced applying the framework to a couple of self-coaching models.

- You've got an idea of who might be the most appropriate to coach at work.

- You've worked out what might get in the way of your coaching at work, and you've created a plan to try to avoid it happening.

- You've reviewed the Essential Questions to ask during some of the most common management discussions in the workplace

- You have an extensive list of coaching questions to apply across any conversation at work

THANK YOU & FINAL THOUGHTS

Before I hand you over to an ever-growing list of great resources to help you achieve even more with your coaching conversations, I want to thank you for buying and reading my book.

I've spent a great deal of time and energy researching and writing it, so it means a lot that you've chosen to spend some of your money on finding out what I learned.

It's the first time I've self-published a book so if there's something you've spotted that you'd like to change or if you have an idea about what else I could include please get in touch by emailing me at kathryn@careerbalance.co.nz

I'd also like to remind you that if you want to use any of the materials or models in here, please remember to check with me first – just to make certain that I honour the permissions I have obtained during my writing process.

I wish you the best of luck with your coaching!

KATHRYN JACKSON FCIPD
PROFILE

BACKGROUND

Kathryn Jackson is a Christchurch based coach with over 20 years of corporate HR, L&D and coaching experience, as of 2017.

Her employment in corporate UK included Andersen's, the Royal Bank of Scotland and Bank of Scotland…where she was responsible for many fundamentals of People Management; designing, delivering and leading initiatives including performance management, succession planning and employee engagement.

Kathryn's business **careerbalance Ltd** has been providing Executive and Leadership Coaching, Career and Outplacement services to NZ businesses for over 10yrs. Clients in the last few years have included CERA, Ernst & Young, CDHB, Noel Leeming Group and for the last four years, SCIRT. She specialises in supporting professionals and leaders who want to build resilience, achieve career success and strive for excellence.

QUALIFICATIONS & PUBLICATIONS

With a commitment to quality, Kathryn has a first class honours degree specialising in HR – with a subsequent post graduate exploration of Motivation at Work. She trained with the Oxford School of Coaching & Mentoring in 2005 and since moving to New Zealand has completed additional training as a Career Coach, DISC and NLP accreditation and most recently an understanding of the Psychology of Goals. In 2017, she completed a six-month European Individual Accreditation with the EMCC and was awarded Senior Practitioner.

Accepted as a Fellow with the CIPD in 2015 it is her continued commitment to CPD that resulted in her decision to research and publish a book about surviving redundancy (a unique journey using a coaching style of writing). This was followed by the book you have just read; aimed at managers who are learning to coach and who want to understand how workplace conversations might sound when they use their new coaching skills. She has just completed a book about building resilience at work, scheduled for publication in 2017/18 by Routledge.

OUTSIDE WORK

Committed to supporting others in a variety of ways, Kathryn has taken part in numerous sporting events to raise money for charity and was actively involved in establishing (and now coaching with) the KEA coaching trust providing coaching to NGO's in New Zealand.

She enjoys life in rural North Canterbury with her family, where she relishes time spent in the saddle of her beloved horses.

E   *kathryn@careerbalance.co.nz*

W   *www.careerbalance.co.nz*

GREAT RESOURCES

The world is full of fantastic coaching resources to help you to achieve your goals in the world of work; here is a selection of some of the most amazing ones that I've found (and which are now well and truly thumbed on my bookshelves!);

BOOKS

Graham Alexander - **Tales from the Top** (UK and US editions) ISBN 978-0785213352

Graham Alexander – **Super Coaching** ISBN 978-1844137015

John Whitmore - **Coaching for Performance** ISBN 9781857883039

Alison Hardingham – **The Coaches Coach** – ISBN 978-1843980759

David Clutterbuck – **Techniques for Coaching & Mentoring** ISBN 978-0750652872

Carol Wilson, John Whitmore, Richard Branson - **Best Practice in Performance Coaching** ISBN 978-0749450823

Ferdinand F. Fournies - **Coaching for improved work performance** –ISBN 978-0071352932

Perry Zeus & Suzanne Skiffington - **The complete guide to coaching at work** ISBN 978-0074708422

David Rock - **Quiet Leadership** ISBN 978-0060835903

Anne Loehr & Brian Emerson - **A managers guide to coaching** ISBN 978-0814409824

Marshall Goldsmith - **Coaching for Leadership** ISBN 978-0787977634

Robert Hargrove - **Masterful Coaching** ISBN 978-0470290354

Harvard School Business Press Pocket - **Coaching People** ISBN 978-1422103470

OTHER STUFF

Coaching At Work – website and online tools

An amazing and very current online resource is available by joining the **Coaching at Work** website. You can choose online membership, or upgrade and receive a regular magazine containing the latest news, tools and resources for coaching in the workplace. For more information go to www.coaching-at-work.com

Allison O'Neill – **The Boss Benchmark** ISBN 978-0473-139506 Do you know what it REALLY takes to be a truly fabulous leader at work? Allison does because she's spent most of her working life as a staff surveyor and in this wonderful little book she shares the 35 ways to reach the Boss Benchmark and then stay there!

Global Coaching Schools

Here are some of the current coaching schools that operate globally in case you'd like to develop your coaching skills even further. They provide a

- **European Mentoring and Coaching Council**: http://www.emccouncil.org/

- **Behavioural Coaching Institute** http://www.behavioral-coaching-institute.com/)

- **International Institute of Coaching** http://www.iicandm.org/

- **International Coaching Council** (http://www.international-coaching-council.com/)

- **International Coach Federation** (http://www.coachfederation.com/ICF/)

- **Worldwide Association of Business Coaches** (http://www.wabccoaches.com/)

The OCM

The Oxford School of Coaching & Mentoring (UK) encourages the development of a wide range of approaches to suit the variety of situations and contexts in which coaching and mentoring takes place. There is no single theoretical coaching model, and the approach has been labelled Situational Coach-Mentoring.

Programmes use a blended learning approach, with access to streamed audio and video content, online measurement tools and social learning activities. All programmes are quality controlled by independent accrediting bodies to ensure that they meet and exceed the most up-to-date professional, occupational and academic standards within the coaching profession.

To find out more go to www.theocm.co.uk

THE SMALL PRINT

At first, I resisted including this section - but on the advice of many I'm going to include it.

I've kept the content of this section as simple as possible and have based it largely on a common-sense approach as opposed to legal speak – I hope you can respect my desire to do so.

All information contained in this book is for informational purposes only; it is not intended as a directive to act. Just because it's written doesn't mean you must say it. It's entirely your choice to use the words in this book or to edit them.

All amendments to the GROW model are with the express written permissions of the creators, Graham Alexander and Sir John Whitmore.

The materials in this book may include information, products and resources from third parties. Where this is the case, I cannot assume any responsibility or liability for any third-party materials or opinions.

In reading this book you agree that neither my company nor I are responsible for the success or failure of your choices and/or conversations because of information presented in it.

No part of these books shall be reproduced, transmitted or sold in whole or in part in any form without prior written consent of the author.

All trademarks and registered trademarks appearing are the property of the respective owners where noted. Images are sourced royalty-free from Pixabay, except for the front cover, which is purchased.

Users of this book are advised to do their own due diligence when making decisions about whether to have a coaching conversation and using the models to develop their teams.

Finally, when having a coaching conversation, please apply common sense (for example; please do not only discuss work-life balance coaching questions with working mothers in your team!).

I honestly hope that you find this book a valuable resource to support you in your coaching conversation toolkit at work. I'd love to know how it contributes to enhancing the conversations that you have at work.

I ask that you respect the time and resources it took for me to write it by encouraging your friends and colleagues to purchase their own copy, should they wish to do so.